LIVE PREPARED!

A layman's view of living a Christian life

Bob Hofmann

authorHOUSE®

AuthorHouse™
1663 Liberty Drive
Bloomington, IN 47403
www.authorhouse.com
Phone: 1-800-839-8640

First published by AuthorHouse   4/8/2011

ISBN: 978-1-4567-3862-4 (sc)
ISBN: 978-1-4567-3861-7 (hc)
ISBN: 978-1-4567-3860-0 (e)

Library of Congress Control Number: 2011901901

Printed in the United States of America

TO THE GLORY OF GOD
AND THE JOYFUL EFFORTS OF
FURTHERING
HIS KINGDOM

CONTENTS

FORWARD

Bob Hofmann has been a faithful and diligent member of my Bible Study group. During the time we have spent together studying God's word I have watched him grow in the knowledge and wisdom of the Lord Jesus Christ. He has also become a dear brother in the Lord and a prayer warrior and partner.

In this book he deals with weighty spiritual matters, but does so in a manner that is not ponderous or theologically intimidating. His relaxed and "folksy" style while making easy reading, conveys deep truths and insights, and at the same time will challenge the reader to seek a closer walk with our Lord and Savior.

I right this short forward with pleasure, and heartily recommend: *Live Prepared: a layman's view of living the life of a Christian.*

Earnest C Seddon Ph.D., Th.D., D.R.E.

PREFACE

Daily, each of us is involved with a plethora of activities aimed at getting us ready for events we know will take place. This includes dressing in certain clothes appropriate for the activities we will be involved in. It entails gathering tools or resources needed to complete an assignment. This list could go on and on. Events in life are all prefaced with what we call preparation. We learn at a young age that to fulfill the tasks and responsibilities of our lives we need to plan and anticipate what is needed to do so.

Preparation calls for thinking, studying, and anticipating everything we will be involved with to complete any task. For example, let's take the simple task of brushing our teeth. To begin we need the items for this task, a brush, toothpaste, and water. But to gather these things we used knowledge of what type of brush and which toothpaste is correct for us. After purchasing these items we put them where they would easily be available, normally in the bathroom, so that is where we go. Next we apply knowledge dealing with the quantity of toothpaste needed. Then we again apply knowledge as to the proper time and procedures to ensure a good job. As you can see even this simple task involves a good deal of preparation. We don't think about it because we have done it so often that it becomes part of our routine. So it should be with living prepared for God.

How sad it is that the very thing for which we were created is the thing few prepare for! To live for the glory of our Heavenly Father is our purpose in life, but all too few ever think of, let alone prepare to do so. We should be in a position every minute of our lives to hear and obey God's call to us, and be ready to face Him upon our deaths, or His coming.

I believe this book contains truths found in scriptures. While reading it ask the Holy Spirit to make those truths open and understandable to you. Through His revelation you will begin to understand your place and purpose in God's eternal plan. When truth is presented, the Spirit will reveal it at the depth you are ready to receive. This is found to be true when reading the Bible. No matter how many times we read scripture, the Spirit will bring something new to light, and we comment, "I've never seen that before!" thus it is with this book. The more times you read it, the more the truths will be revealed.

Questions are provided after each chapter to stimulate personal reflection or group discussion.

The use of masculine pronouns found here is not intended to be gender specific, but just for ease in writing.

Bob Hofmann

ACKNOWLEDGEMENTS

I wish to begin my list of people of have taught and encouraged me with my parents, Clarence and Clara Hofmann. They provided a secure home and positive direction to me with the blessing of leading me to know God by having me baptized and taking me to church regularly. Next, I wish to thank the Nazarene minister whose name is since forgotten, who took several young boys to an also forgotten traveling evangelist where I first totally admitted by sins, was forgiven, and felt for the first time the personal love and peace of Jesus Christ.

After my rebellious and inattentive period from late teens to marriage, God graced me with meeting an Episcopal Priest and his wonderful wife, Fr Chuck and Bernice Mitchell, who taught and lead me into a deep, personal relationship with God, and to love Him and His people dearly. Those who were in this fellowship at the same time have become some of my dearest friends and brothers and sisters in Christ, and their love and support has been my constant companion ever since.

Numerous fellow believers have touched my life and to all those I hope that I may have touched them for the Lord in return. I wish to acknowledge Fr John Naumann who has exemplified sacrificial giving for me and many others. Fr Jacob Knee is the current rector of the church I attend and has provided inspired leadership to bring his congregation into a loving relationship one to another and with God. I also wish to thank Don and Vivian Westall for their continuing support and encouragement in the writing of this book. Last but certainly not least, I wish to thank and acknowledge Earnest and Cynthia Seddon for their generous gifts of love, prayer, support, and knowledge which have enabled me to finish this work.

All praise, glory, and honor I give to our most high and glorious God for giving me the inspiration, knowledge, support, and ability to complete this undertaking in what I hope will be a lifetime of answering His call.

1.

PREPARE TO DIE!

"Prepare to Die" or "prepare to meet your maker" is not just some cheesy line from a second rate movie, it is a proposal which needs to be at the top of our priority list. We all seek to delay the final act of our lives which we all will experience, the death of our mortal bodies. Death is the thing which we should have been preparing for as soon as we were old enough to understand what death means. But, do we really understand what death is? To most people death is the end. It is a barrier they feel is impenetrable, a concept so terrifying that is best put off for as long as possible. Most people in western culture do not talk about it, even though everyone thinks about it. It is not politically correct to converse about that one thing we all are racing toward, and fear prevents the mentioning of it even to our closest friends. We pretend that it will never happen to us, "it only happens to the weak and elderly." It is something we avoid talking about even as we see friends and loved ones dying. Yet most people are so fascinated by death that the obituary page in the local paper is one of the most read sections. Often, preparing for death is an activity delayed until the last minute because preparing brings it to the forefront of our thoughts, which to most is very unnerving.

    To Christians death is a transition, a leaving of our mortal bodies to enter the spiritual realm, and then someday to return to a perfected physical body.[1] It is a time of both sorrow and joy. It is at the same time leaving

1   1 Corinthians 15:51

those we love behind, and having a glorious meeting with our Heavenly Father and His Son, our Savior Jesus Christ. It causes the survivors left behind to consider unrealized dreams and ambitions left by the deceased, but it will also be a wonderful reunion with departed loved ones, and all the saints who have passed before us. To the Christian, death is neither dreaded nor sought. It is a part of the life which has been surrendered to the Designer and Maker to fulfill His eternal plan for us.

To many non Christians, death is a fearful mystery. Some non Christians believe that there is nothing after this life, and the grave is as far as they will venture. Their motto is; "go for all you can get now while you are able." Others are not sure what to expect, but "they have been good people all their lives and if there is a God, he will surely reward them for their good deeds." Still others have not yet seen the need to form an opinion, and will take whatever comes. Finally, there are those who believe in reincarnation. They expect to come back in one form or another to try and live a better, more perfect life.

As we near that dreaded, universal event, we all understand the necessity of concluding financial and material affairs. Bidding our friends and loved ones good bye becomes a high priority if we are given a chance to do so. We are adept at these things because the world holds them as important. Every attorney, banker, or financial consultant will jump at the opportunity to help finalize our assets before our demise (for a small fee of course.) Anyone on the street can offer his advice as to what we need to do. But, after we are dead does that really matter? If we are in eternal agony in the fires of hell will it matter that we wisely distributed our wealth in the most equitable way? As our children spend their inheritance while we are suffering terribly from the absence of all that is good, with out any chance of relief, will it comfort us to know that the best legal minds in town agree with the content and form of our will? Certainly it won't. Life is but a quick flash in the midst of eternity. Everything we do in that short moment called life will have ramifications stretching throughout eternity. This is the reason we must seek to gain the promise of eternal life while we are able.

WE HAVE A CHOICE

The truth is, we were created to belong to God! He conceived us and has a place in His eternal plan for us. With this knowledge, we have two choices. We can believe that we are indeed the property of the Creator of the universe, or we can reject Him, and become sons of Satan.[2] If we believe the former, we have aligned ourselves with Him that called the universe into being, created this world and all its inhabitants, and holds the future in His hand. We have chosen our Heavenly Father who is Love, and submit ourselves to Him and His wonderful grace. God knew us and had a plan for us to fulfill before creation began. He made us to have a close, loving relationship with Him which will last all through this life, and forever.

If we choose the latter and reject God, we choose to be His enemy and align ourselves with Satan, who rejected Him first. God will discard these as unnecessary and unsuitable for heaven. He has that right for He is sovereign. We are His desire whether we will acknowledge it or not, but He allows the choice to be ours. He is a just God and every decision he makes is also equally just.

EVIDENCE FOR GOD

Some say there is no God. Any who say that must be blind and deaf.[3] They must never have seen a beautiful lake while walking in the mountains, or watched the sun set from the seashore. They must never have heard the love songs of a hundred different birds, or the crackling of a campfire. They must have been oblivious to the intricate relationships between the plants and animals of an ecosphere. They must never have studied the complexity of the human body. In short they have *decided* to discount the reality of God.

Throughout history, mankind has believed in a superior being. Even to this day primitive people in the most remote parts of the world believe in a god, or gods. Since the fall from grace, mankind has had a deep hunger that is satisfied only by the belief of a higher power. We have a longing in our hearts to be part of some larger plan, something which on our own, we could not achieve, nor even attempt. Life is unfulfilling without reason and purpose greater than mere living. Belonging and loving motivates our desires to be in relationships, while hoping for strength and protection from this hostile world. Relationships all fall short of the one we were created by and created for. Loneliness, fear, and separation can only be resolved through a relationship with the One who knows us completely and still loves us unconditionally.

---

2   John 8:44
3   Psalm 14:11

THE DIFFERENCE OF CHRISTIANITY

All modern religions except one have major principle in common. Mankind strives to reach or become god through our own efforts. By striving to behave in certain moralistically acceptable patterns or good works, mankind hopes to achieve a closeness, or even equality to god. Doing great quantities of charitable deeds is believed to be the way mankind can reach great heights. Some religions will even give multiple chances. Sin terribly in this life? Don't worry; perhaps we can do better in the next life. We can stay on that merry-go-round until we get it right. Other religions may also say that god is already in us. We just need to uncover our own divine nature to be god. Christians believe that this thinking is flawed to say the least. This is the same thinking that caused the fall of mankind in the Garden of Eden and will lead to our eternal separation from God.

The exception to the rule of working for our salvation and our own greatness is Christianity. Christians believe that a loving, holy, and just God created the entire universe. He also created mankind in His image so they could have a close relationship. Because of His perfect love, it was His joy and desire to bring us into existence to be in a close, loving relationship with Him in a setting of incredible beauty. Because of God's love, we do not strive to reach His level. Instead, He reaches down to us and pleads for us to come to Him and all He offers. Nothing we can do or say can erase the stain that sin has left on us, and we deserve punishment and death. In His eternal justice with mercy God offers us the free gift of salvation, for it is only by His free offering of grace that we can be freed from the consequence of sin.[4]

The Christian God is all knowing, all powerful, and is present throughout His entire creation. He is love. That doesn't mean that love is just a characteristic he exhibits, but it means that His purpose, will, nature, and eternal intentions are love. God is also holy. Again it is not just a characteristic God possesses, but it defines His nature. God is the definition of perfection, and therefore everything about Him is holy. God has set in place for His creation a list of rules. In His sovereignty He, as architect and builder of the universe, institutes laws which fulfill His plan for the order He establishes. Thereby, He is the eternal judge and dispenser of justice.

---

4   1 John 1:9

IN THE BEGINING

When God had finished creation and Adam and Eve inhabited God's perfect garden, God set down His rules to them. It was not terribly complicated. Eat of every plant in the garden, even from the tree of life, except one. As we all know that tree bore the fruit which purportedly contained the knowledge of good and evil. All Adam had to do was cultivate and protect the garden, and obey by not eating the forbidden fruit. Eve just needed to be his devoted helpmate. God so desired to take care of them that He provided not only everything they needed, but also everything they wanted. [5]

The forbidden fruit that they ate was no magical elixir, and its flesh did not suddenly give knowledge to them. They became aware of the difference between good and evil. They had already known good, that is they knew God intimately, but now they discovered evil. Disobedience removed them from their position with God, and anything outside God and His will is innately evil. Their disobedience of God's statute not to eat of that particular tree was evil, and by doing so they experienced the full force of consequences it produced.

Imagine yourself in the situation of never needing to worry about where to sleep that would be exposed to the weather. The temperature was always perfect and it never rained in God's garden, for the garden was watered from a river which came up from the ground.[6] Imagine never needing to worry about food, for it surrounded them in abundance. Imagine never being afraid, never being sick, never being upset or angry for any reason, and never having to worry about death. Imagine the privilege of being in close commune with the Founder of all creation. Life could not have been better, yet man was not content. Man was greedy and full of pride. Man, the crown of God's creation wanted to be god. So by his disobedience, man drew the righteous anger of God and separated himself from His presence.

Another consequence of the fall of mankind is the curse put upon the land. Instead of having plants that produced abundant food with no effort, man suddenly had to work to provide the food and shelter needed to sustain himself. Mankind's life would now be finite, and would now be spent in constant work and worry instead of communing with God.[7]

---

5   Genesis 2:15-17
6   Genesis 2:6
7   Genesis 3:17-19

GOD'S NATURAL LAWS

God made the universe and everything in it. He desired the things He created and He had the power, wisdom, and ability to accomplish that task. That means He also desired mankind. God dearly desires each one of us. Each individual has a purpose and plan for his life which is only realized by submission to the will and plan of God.

God set all natural laws and principles to regulate how creation functions. This natural order is without exception or choice. The relationship of interstellar bodies to one another is not flexible. The force of gravity and the laws of physics are as constant today as they were during creation. On Earth, the plants have no option as to where they grow or how they look, they follow the laws God has set forth. What man sows, he shall also reap. If we plant grain we do not harvest fruit but the same in-kind plants we expect. The same is true for animals. A pair of horses does not produce birds. Animals do not prepare and plan to gather food; they respond to instinct and follow the nature of their creation.

There is an exception to the rule which allows no choice and no option. That exception is God's dearest creation, mankind. Since God created us in His image to have a close relationship with Him, He gave us free will. God wanted such a close fellowship with all humanity that He wanted us to *choose* to be in that relationship. God loved us so much that He wanted us to return that love to the point of being in union with Him, not by force or coercion but by realizing perfect love and loving in return.

We, being curious creatures by His design, are continually investigates God's creation and its laws. We call this science. God gave us inquisitive minds to explore and seek to understand our surroundings. God allows this to show His mighty power, wisdom, and glory. Through our discoveries we learn the greatness and majesty of God and thereby give Him glory and honor. The more we learn about the unbelievable intricacies of God's creation, the more we understand that it is not by chance or evolution that it exists.

God could have put mankind into the same position as the rest of creation, that is, having no choice in life, but that was not and is not God's will. God desires us to love and choose Him, as much as God loves and chooses us. God wanted (and still wants) to supply all our needs, and be the loving Father to us all, bringing glory to Himself in doing so. If we choose to love Him and be obedient, He will supply our every need and oh, so much more!

God never hid from Adam and Eve the consequence of disobedience.

He made it clear that all the benefits of living in the garden, and communing with Him would be lost by disobedience, and death would be the ultimate conclusion to a life filled with fear, misery, and back-breaking toil.

From the very beginning we failed to understand the depth of God's goodness and love. In our greed and lust for autonomy we chose to disobey God. We wanted not just to be the select of all creation, but to be equal with the Creator. Coveting God's place of honor we tried to be our own gods and worship our selves. It was our "right" to live as we chose. We allowed our egos to be inflated by the deceptive urgings of the Evil One, and fell from grace.

To show the futility of life without Him, God allowed us to live the life of our choosing. We descended to the lowest pits of immorality until God finally said that He would destroy the world with a great flood. God chose the only remaining righteous man, Noah and his family to start over. God again tried to show the lack of an abundant and fulfilling life for mankind without Him, but to the same results. Mankind failed miserably. God created us and knew the only way we could have all He desired was through the intimate love He offered and responding to His call. God was showing mankind the utter futility of leading our own life apart from Him, but mankind would not accept the truth.

The good news is that God has provided redemption from this accursed life. He again offers us a choice. We can either accept His grace or die both physically and spiritually.

POINTS TO PONDER

1. Why is death called the last enemy?

2. Am I afraid of death? If so why? If not why?

3. What does "die to self – alive to Christ" mean?

2.

PREPARE TO LIVE!

Time has no bounds for the glorious and eternal God. He knew of the downfall of humanity before the universe was created. Even with this foreknowledge, God's desire was to create us to be the object of His great love. He had already conceived the plan to bring glory and honor to Himself and redemption to all people before the original sin was committed. He set in motion a plan which would restore creation back to its original status, free from the curse of sin, and back to the state of eternal love. God intended for all to live a rich, full life in close relationship with Him while experiencing all of His bounty. It was painful for God to see mankind struggle and toil to eke out meager living. God created us to live a life of abundance, not one of just survival, so He began His plan of redemption.

GOD'S MAN

In His unceasing love for all humanity even after its fall from grace, God still revealed Himself to righteous men, and blessed them with having a relationship with Him. One such man was Abraham. He was a man who loved, obeyed, and served God, and had faith in God and His promises. Because of his faith and love for God, Abraham was the man with whom God chose to make a covenant. God promised to make

Abraham's descendants as numerous as the stars in the sky, and bless all the families of the world through him.

God chose Abraham's progeny to be His people, a nation to which He would reveal His laws and ordinances. He would be their God and they would be His people, a nation of priests through whom the world could come to know God. These people are known as the Hebrew people of Israel. God wanted to use His people to show the rest of the world His glory, power and love. He was going to make them a nation of priests to gather the rest of the world to His altar to reveal His loving kindness, great mercies and eternal righteousness.

GOD'S ORDINANCES

Since Adam and Eve had disobeyed God, humanity now had the knowledge of good and evil. God needed to enlighten them to the laws He ordained through which, by obedience, they were acceptable before Him. These laws were to show once again that left unto our selves, we are sinful creatures incapable of doing good and continually choosing to do evil.[8] We are enemies of God and are constantly in rebellion against Him. Because of this, everyone is bound for eternal damnation, being eternally separated from our Creator.

God gave His laws and ordinances to us through Moses, a descendant of Abraham. These laws dealt with the proper way to relate to God, how to relate to each other, and to show us our true position in His plan. Failure to abide with these laws or commandments resulted in mankind being guilty of sin, and suffering separation from God. He used these laws to reveal that left unto our selves we can not be righteous and are deserving of death. Again, because God loves mankind so much, He provided a means by which our sin could be forgiven. This was the blood of a sacrificed animal, usually a young lamb or bullock, and the presentation of its blood on the altar of God. The life of the animal was in the blood,[9] and sin required that death be the penalty.[10]

God continually reached out to mankind, calling us back to His intended purpose by offering His great mercy. Speaking through the prophets, God always pleaded for His people to turn from their evil ways and seek Him, promising to provide His forgiveness, providence, and protection from earthly and spiritual harm. These lessons are preserved

---

8   Romans 7:7-13
9   Leviticus 17:11
10   Romans 6:23

in the inspired word of God, the Holy Bible, for all generations. The Israelites were a stubbornly rebellious and forgetful people continually turning their backs on God even after He freed them from their bondage in Egypt by performing miracles before them. This rebellion eventually led to the destruction of their beloved city Jerusalem and exile into foreign countries.

GOD'S PLAN OF SALVATION

In His perfect timing, God instituted His plan for salvation and redemption for all mankind. God came unto us in human form[11] to become the sacrificial lamb[12] to take upon Himself the sins of the world. He was fully God and fully human. His name was, and is, Jesus the Christ. Being fully human He experienced all the emotions, doubts, temptations, and pain all men endure, and being fully God he had the exclusive ability to be the mediator between heaven and earth, between the spiritual and material realms. He lived His entire life within the limits of God's laws, that is, He was without sin. His close fellowship with God, His heavenly father, and the Holy Spirit was His source of wisdom and strength as he completely surrendered Himself to God's will.

Early in His ministry, Jesus gathered a group of followers to teach and prepare to spread the good news of the love of God and His plan of redemption for mankind to all nations. Jesus taught with remarkable authority and clarity which astounded the clerical hierarchy of the day. He preformed miracles and wonders before His followers showing the awesome power of God and the truth of His message, as well as revealing His true identity. He was obedient and submitted to His Father even to His death, which was the purpose for His descent to Earth. For it was God's plan to bring creation back to perfect order and make possible the closeness of a loving relationship between Him and mankind. Jesus' death was the sacrifice that made this possible. It was the blood of Jesus Christ shed for all of mankind that took away all sin,[13] won victory over death,[14] and opened the pathway to God the father.[15] His blood not only atoned for all the sins ever committed, but also broke the bond of sin that had imprisoned mankind.

---

11   Matthew 1:23
12   Revelations 13:8
13   1 John 1:7
14   1 Corinthians 15:57
15   John 14:6

Jesus' death, however, is far from being the end of the story. The mighty power of God was again displayed in the resurrection of Jesus, and His ascension into heaven was the means by which we, who are in Christ, have the authority to fulfill His commission. His resurrection and ascension into heaven also broke the ultimate grip of Satan on creation. Death itself was defeated by this mighty act of God, providing the doorway of eternal life with Him to all who believe and put their trust and faith in Jesus Christ.

God provided the only way of coming to Him and that way is Jesus Christ.[16] He made it clear that salvation through Christ's death was a free gift,[17] and nothing mankind could do on its own would ever be sufficient to atone for its sins. We on our own are corrupt and evil, hating and continually rejecting God. Nothing we do can begins to pay the huge debt that we owe for our sin, for we have all sinned and fallen short[18] of our intended place in God's plan. Jesus said that no man goes to the Father except through Him, by means of His death upon the cross. Thus, all are condemned to eternal separation or in other words hell unless they believe in Jesus, and that His death is the atonement for sin.

RECEIVE SALVATION

When Jesus ascended to heaven, God did not abandon us. He sent His Holy Spirit to dwell within us. The Holy Spirit's task, in part, is to convict us of sin, unrighteousness, and judgment, and to bring us to the Lord Jesus Christ. By this, Jesus Christ is proven to be the only means of salvation and His name is exalted and glorified.

To receive eternal life with God and the Lord Jesus Christ, one needs to believe that Jesus is the Son of God who died on the cross to atone for the sins of the whole world; that each person is sinful and agree with God that their sin is deserving of death; that an amending of life by turning from sin and toward God is required: that Jesus Christ was raised from the dead, and ascended with authority to heaven; and ask Him to become the Lord of our lives by surrendering to him.

To choose to accept Jesus Christ one needs to trust in the eternal love of God the father. He has given us so many examples of His love and bounty that they are often taken for granted. He has given us life and elements needed to continue life. He provides air to breath, food for nourishment,

16   Acts 4:12
17   Romans 6:23
18   Romans 3:23

and water to drink. He has given us family and friends to associate with to alleviate our loneliness. He has blessed each of us with special gifts and talents with a mind and body to serve our needs. He has provided the beautiful and bountiful earth to provide for us. All good things have come through God and yet we hesitate to put our faith and trust in Him. In whom will we trust if not Him? Will we rely on our corrupt human nature? Will we trust in the great deceiver Satan? Surely all we need to do is examine our world that surrounds us to see that God is the great I Am, and that He alone is worthy of our trust.

NEW CREATURES

If we choose God and His free gift of salvation through His son, God will begin the task of transforming us into new creatures. If we will choose to give up the wrong thoughts of being autonomous and surrender all we are to God, He will give us blessings beyond what we can hope for. He will then turn us from the natural ways of serving ourselves, yielding to the corruption of the world, and being led into rebellion through the temptations of Satan and his demons. When we surrender our lust for fame, power, and pride and begin to love God for whom He is, we begin to love all His creation, especially man, with the love shown to us by God.

God sends the third person of the Holy Trinity of God, the Holy Spirit, to assist in our transformation and to help us to grow in union with Him. We have the very nature of God and His Son Jesus within us. At this point a task of the Holy Spirit is to take control of our desires and passions, and guide us toward the fulfillment of His plan. He begins our transformation from sinful man into the likeness of Jesus Christ.[19]

There are literally thousands of books and articles describing in great detail the truths written here. There will certainly be thousands more, unless Christ comes back before they can be written. Nearly every one who reads this has heard about salvation through Jesus Christ, but few have completely surrendered their lives and have become restored through the incredible mercy of God. If you are one who has not heard the gospel of peace, or have not fully surrendered all that you are to Him, please take these words to heart right now and begin the greatest journey of your life. It is free for the asking!

The most important idea I hope to pass on to you in this chapter is the personal call God makes to each individual. This call requires an equally

---

19   Romans 8:29

personal response. Even though Christ died for the sin of the world, your response must be a very personal one. Christ died for *you!* Christ suffered so that *you* may be healed. *You* must receive Him as Savior, Lord, and King. Being part of any fellowship or church will not assure your salvation. The family into which you were born will not ensure your salvation. Listening to Christian radio, and even praying diligently does not mean that you are saved. He calls us to realize our pitiful state of rebellion and wretched sinfulness, to humbly ask for forgiveness for sins, and to be washed clean by the blood of Christ, realizing who He is and completely surrendering to Him. He calls us to relinquish our desires and plans and begin to relish the far superior plan God has for us. The instant we do these things, God has promised to begin the transformation which will make us into a new creation. God has promise to give us His Holy Spirit[20] to empower us to become the new people[21] He desired and planned for us to be; to live a life that is blessed and fulfilled; and to partake in the blessing of eternal life with Him.

The decision to accept Jesus Christ as Lord and Savior requires us to have absolute trust in His love, motive, and ability. He truly is who He says He is. He has undying love, compassion, and mercy for all, and beckons us to come to Him. He has the power to create the entire universe and control everything, even death. Absolute trust in Him is the only way to receive all that He has for us.

FIRST STEPS

The continuation of our transformation leads us to be baptized. By doing so, we are making a formal and public pronouncement of our desire to live within the realm of God. Several things occur by being baptized. We receive the power of the Holy Spirit, and have Him residing within us. We are marked as Christ's own, and no power can displace Christ as our source. We also commit to be part of the body of Christ, His church and partake in His sacraments.

Being baptized is an act of obedience to the great commission given by Jesus Christ. Emerging from the water of baptism is symbolic of the resurrection of Jesus. Some denominations believe in the baptism of only mature people, while others baptize infants also. The physical manner in

---

20   Acts 1:8
21   2 Corinthians 5:17

14

which the baptism is done is less important than the spiritual reality that transpires at that moment.

If we are baptized as a child we receive that same membership into the family and body of Christ as our parents have decided for us. But at some point after reaching maturity and being able to make decisions on our own, (the age of accountability, usually around the age of 12 or 13) we must renew our baptismal vows for ourselves. This is often done by participating in the rite of confirmation. In the baptism of a baby, all the gifts of God and privileges of being His child have already been given, and a personal choice is all that is needed. Indeed, choosing to follow Jesus must be a personal choice and surrendering to Him can only come from within our hearts.

By attending church regularly, we begin to learn the role the church plays in the lives of its congregation, its role in God's plan, and how the church impacts the community and the world for Christ. All the rich traditions and teachings begin to make sense as the Spirit reveals the truth about them to us. By becoming united in the body of Christ, we learn the value each member is to one another and to God's eternal plan. God created us to be relational both with Him and with one another, and to love both dearly.

When we have begun this process we will be "prepared to die", and "prepared to live". From that time on, nothing in the universe can separate us from the love of God.[22] If we choose not to accept God's remarkable free gift of salvation we should begin to prepare to spend eternity in hell. This is the undeniable truth. There is no middle ground. We are either bound for eternity in heaven or hell.

POINTS TO PONDER

1. Is there a difference between "existing" and "living".

2. Jesus said "because I live you shall live also". What does this mean?

3. In what way IS Jesus life?

---

22   Romans 8:35

4.

3.

PREPARE TO CHANGE!

In the first chapter death was discussed. That death is the death of our bodies, since our souls and spirits are eternal. At the time of this death our mortal bodies are separated from our eternal, spiritual parts. We can and must experience another death of our own choosing and desire. This death is the dying to all the forces that appose the nature, desire, and will of God. This includes the self-seeking and self-serving sinful nature which led to mankind's downfall and continues to separate us from God, as well as the temptation and influence used by principalities, rulers of darkness, and spiritual wickedness in high places[23] to entice us away from Him. By our nature we are sinful creatures capable of committing appalling acts against God and all His creation, especially other humans. These include acts of commission, all which we should not do, and omission, the failure to do that which we ought. By our nature we make ourselves God's enemy and our vile wickedness is released upon all creation. Pride rears its ugly head temping us to elevate ourselves to God's status, causing us to justify our actions, and clouding our minds from the truth. Our best efforts and human goodness are filth when compared to God's standards of holy perfection[24].

By seeking and choosing God's help, we can put these things that separate us from Him, to literal death. The Holy Spirit reveals our evil

23   Ephesians 6:12
24   See Isaiah 64:6

ways to us so we can continually choose to turn from them, ignoring their alluring pull and thereby putting them to death, thus defusing their wicked power. We hang these actions of sin on the cross with Jesus Christ and there the bond of sin is broken, freeing all who partake in God's salvation from their wicked power for ever. We are in the Lord Jesus Christ and also partake in his death, causing the grip of evil[25] and sin to be slain. This in part is the daily picking up of our cross of which Jesus spoke. A season of change will then surely begin in us.

DYING TO OURSELVES

God has set forth laws that provide for life coming into being as a result of death. An example used by Christ in the Bible is a seed. All plant seeds must "die" to their old form upon being planted in the ground[26]. New life then springs forth and bears much more of like produce. Our lives as Christians parallel this truth. Until we choose to die to our own will, the desires of the world, and the evil powers of this universe, God will not recreate us into that new creature that bears fruit. The desire to accomplish this comes as we begin to change into the new creature filled with, and directed by the Holy Spirit. He shows us every area of our life that misses the will of God, and by His love we begin to despise it, even that which we often did and enjoyed. These acts become disgusting to us and we try to avoid them like the death they bring. Our weakness because of our nature sometimes causes us to fall back to evil ways, but His eternal mercy is shown as we again repent and turn back to Him. As we become new beings, we become more knowledgeable in discerning the luring call of evil forces and resist the temptations they flaunt, as we turn to the power of the Holy Spirit.

Jesus told Nicodemus, "I tell you the truth, no one can see the kingdom of God unless he is born again[27]." Jesus was explaining the way death was necessary to rid mankind of the carnal nature he is born with. The rebirth is the redeemed man choosing to proceed with the life now available in Christ, which is free from the bondage of sin and death. Man's new source is spiritual from the spiritual realm of God. Mortal mankind cannot approach God by temporal means, but only by the spirit that God supplies. As natural childbirth is the radical changing of status, so is the new birth brought about by the indwelling of the Holy Spirit.

25   Romans 6:3-7
26   John 12:24
27   John 3:3

A NEW CREATURE

By our dying and rebirth we become new creatures which resemble Jesus Christ, the only man that knew and lived in the true nature of God, because He is God. Through the power of the Holy Spirit, God has given us the ability to change our desires and decisions, and choose to live as Christ did. His life of loving and serving others brought glory and honor to His Father in heaven, and His total commitment and reliance on God set the standard for us to follow. Christ's close union with God the Father is the opportunity for us to see and implement that perfect example. Such acts bring us into His favor and restore our real position with Him.

Obedience, however, is not enough. Compliance and total obedience to God's laws and commandments of our own will is superficial and virtually impossible. It takes the power of the Holy Spirit to continue our transformation toward the likeness of Jesus. We cannot win this battle on our own. God intended this so mankind can not boast that by our own will or ability we have conquered the power of sin. As we learn to rely completely on Him by surrendering everything we are and all we have to the will and authority of God, totally trusting Him, His divine grace molds us into Christ's image. It is by surrendering our lives and abandoning our wills to His that we gain a full and complete life toward the perfection of God's plan for us. It is in total surrendering to God's love that the avenue to our purpose of life and ability to thrive in it is opened. To love the Lord with all out hearts, (the core of our being, our spirit), all our soul, (our emotions) all our minds, (our thoughts) and strength, (our bodies) is to completely surrender to Him.

Desiring our transformation, we yearn to learn more of God, and long to gain the wisdom this knowledge provides. We seek Him with all of our ability, by starting to look for Him in very aspect of our lives, and in His creation around us. We seek Him in our church services and in every line of the scriptures we read. During our search, we begin to realize that God has always been there and yet we have not seen Him. We discover that He has first loved and sought us and welcomes our attempts to find Him. As we find God and learn His will, we begin to accept it and change by applying it in our lives. When His will becomes our will, all the power and promises of God become available to us.

God's will is an extension of His desire. He desires that His creation would once again be free from sin, and the curse that sin brought with it. He desires man to choose Him, and love and obey Him. God desires man to worship Him in spirit and in truth and love those that share in the body of Christ. He also desires for everything to willfully come under the authority given to Jesus Christ. But, we can never worship in spirit and in truth until we have the Holy Spirit who reveals all truth.

SEEKING GOD AND HIS TRUTH

God reveals Himself through many channels. We continually seek and learn His truth, for learning the truth brings us into a working ability to know God and willingly partake in the mission He gives us. Upon discovering any part of God's truth, we should be teachable and open our hearts and minds to receive and implement it. Remember, truth will set us free. Jesus also said that He is the way, the truth, and the life[28]. Maturing as Christians involves seeking, finding, and implementing God's truth in our lives. As it is written: knock and the door shall be opened. Seek and we shall find. Ask and it will be given.[29]

The primary way God reveals truth is through His written word, the Holy Bible. Devout people throughout many generations have documented, through divine revelation, God's relationship with His people and the history of the effect this has had on their lives. Through this testimony we begin to learn the nature and character of God, and see His plan for all as He unveils it in His timing. He has shown through the centuries every circumstance that can befall mankind, and the faults and weaknesses we possess. God has also shown the greatness of His power acted out through the men and women who have remained devout to Him; great military battles through David, incalculable wisdom and wealth through Solomon, and unswerving obedience and love through Ruth and Esther.

In the scriptures great men of prophecy have spoken for God to His people and have laid the framework for things to come so we are prepared to see and understand His actions as they transpire, or have already transpired. Such is the example of the coming of Jesus Christ. The Old Testament abounds with the promises of God to send a savior, and free His people. A loving King to lead God's people. Inspired men have declared God's mercy and loving compassion through countless examples given of confession of sin and repentance by turning to Him. Scripture reveals God's plan and promises not only for Israel, but also all who turn to Him, acknowledging Him as their God.

In God's perfect timing, He sent his only begotten son, Jesus Christ to

28   John 14:6
29   Matthew 7:7

live as one of us and give us living testimony of the nature and will of God the Father. God himself through Jesus Christ came to speak and exhibit directly to man the truth that leads to fulfillment of this life and life eternal with Him. He gave us an intimate look at all His divine attributes and nature. These things are written in the New Testament of the Holy Bible, bringing a clear and lasting example of God and His loving grace.

God is eternal, the same yesterday, today, and forever.[30] Time has no bounds on Him. As it is written, a thousand years are as a day to Him.[31] Therefore these truths are as real and relevant today as they were when written, and as they will be until Christ returns and all prophesies are fulfilled.

ALWAYS TEST THE TRUTH

Truth comes also from mature members of the body of Christ. Whether this is a pastor, a mentor, or someone who has the gift of prophecy makes little difference as long as their message aligns itself with the truths we have already learned and those shown through the Bible. Truths can be delivered through teachings and Bible studies. Books can also be a great source of God's truth in any number of topics, including all the written traditions of the church. Simply attending a good church with a Bible believing pastor, and listing to sermons not only will bring wisdom, but also the means of applying that wisdom in our lives. Participating regularly in church services is instructional in the ways of worshiping. Studying ancient creeds and articles of faith written by earlier saints establishes a solid foundation for our personal knowledge.

Perhaps the best source of growth and learning is by asking questions through dialog with a mentor. Spending time with any mature Christian will result in growth if we are eager to learn, teachable, and truly desire to change. The Holy Spirit will enlighten our hearts and minds to His truths as we hear it proclaimed from all of these sources.

It is said that a person can find God through the intricacies of creation. The gloriousness of His creation is seen through all the diverse yet interwoven ecosystems in which each member plays an important part. Every little detail of the world is thought out and planned. Such a glorious and detailed plan has an equally glorious and detailed Planner.[32]

In the study to know and understand our Glorious God, we need to be

30   Hebrews 13:8
31   Psalms 90:4
32   Romans 1:19 ff

ever vigilant to ensure we are learning truth. A false prophet by his greed and lust for power can present enough truth as to be believable, but his message is self serving and full of traps to ensnare those it can. The result of this type of fraud is to draw us into trusting and obeying him, not to lead us into a deeper relationship with our heavenly Father. If any presentation does not continue to point our hearts toward the Father, Son, and Holy Spirit we need to ignore and reject that teaching.

Our eternal adversary Satan also strives to throw us off the path that leads to eternal life and giving ourselves to God. He is the great deceiver and knows our every weakness with which he hopes to lead us astray. Only the continual balancing of new information with what we have already learned and what the Bible says will prevent our departure from the road which leads us home to God.

Because God is totally sovereign, no one should ever try to limit what He can, or may do. No one should ever place a time table or other obstacle on how God plans to act. He has set His plan in motion and will continue to implement it through to completion. His plan was developed before the beginning of time, and detailed as to how each situation would play out. All these things add to the knowledge and truth of God's almighty and holy nature, and gives us better understanding as to our response to Him, as well as a reverence for His awesomeness.

When we first accepted Jesus Christ as our personal Lord and Savior we began to change. Having received the Holy Spirit upon our conversion, we are a new creature from that point on.[33] The process is not instantaneous for our minds and we must continue to grow in the grace and knowledge of our Lord Jesus Christ.[34] The more we learn of Him, the more we continue to change. Being in a relationship with God results in change, and if we do not change it is impossible to continue to have a relationship with Him. God's deep love for us compels us to look to Him for His grace, and being so deeply loved even as sinners, draws us to respond to Him in ways that are uncommon to us. We begin to reprioritize everything in our lives, through the prompting of the Holy Spirit, and bring them in line with God's priorities.

---

33   2 Corinthians 5:17
34   2 Peter 3:18

EXPERIENCING GOD

All these ways of discovering truth will teach us about God. They provide a solid basis for our beliefs and show us that we are secure in putting our unswerving faith in Him. However, knowing about God is secondary to knowing Him personally. We can learn about the ocean and become educated about every detail known to man about it. We can look at pictures, study scientific observations, and listen to others who have been to the ocean. We can learn of the marine plant life, and be amazed at the vast variety of its animals. We can marvel at the vastness and depth to which its waters fall. These things are valuable to prepare us to experience the ocean ourselves, but fall far short of completely immersing ourselves in it. We need to *experience* all the sights, smells, and even the salty taste of the water to begin to fully appreciate the uniqueness of that environment. We must use all our God given senses, and our intellect and imagination to fully understand this part of creation. So it is with God.

Most people have a grand vision of what they want in life. Most Americans have the dream of having a home, family, and a job which provides for these things and more. Others in less prosperous countries may just want to have shelter and enough food to get through the day. Still others live in constant fear. Many do not have any freedom and liberty, and live under tyranny. Regardless of man's circumstances, the hopes and dreams he has are shallow and pale compared to the perfect plan of God. We will be much better off when we forfeit our own plans and replaced them with God's plan for us.

NEW PRIORITIES WITH PATIENCE

We realize that this life is temporary, and we should begin to store up riches in heaven by serving, worshipping, and obeying God. Years are spent in a futile effort to acquire riches, fame, or any of a million vices, yet none of them can give the lasting peace and fulfillment that God can give. Sadly, few are willing to set aside their dreams to obtain the ultimate. We settle for mediocrity rather than believing and striving for God's best that He holds for us. The lies and temptations of Satan and the world are a constant hindrance to man's believing and receiving God's abundance. But those who are willing to change their hopes and dreams to those of the Lord's will have the blessings of God in this life and the bliss of eternal life with Him.

Mankind has always wanted instant gratification. Even in the Garden of Eden we wanted instant power and stature. This is still lived out today. We want to lose weight *now*. We want an education *now*. We want a new house, car, or whatever suits our fancy *now*. We should not be so short sighted. Everything has a season, and God will act at exactly the right moment. When we fail to see God's actions we think He doesn't care, or that we are not worthy of His response. That is generally the time that He is busy laying the foundation for our growth and continuing blessings. If we always remember that He loves us so much that while we were very terrible sinners He sent His Beloved Son to die in our place[35], how could we ever doubt that He doesn't care or that we are unworthy? How could we ever doubt that our Father Who gave us His precious Son would withhold anything we need?

If we first seek the kingdom of God and His righteousness, the need for food, shelter, and all the necessities of life will be added to us.[36] This kingdom is not necessarily a place, but rather it involves putting Jesus Christ as lord over all we are and all we possess. The kingdom is where the king reigns. In this case the kingdom is within us for when we acknowledge Him as our sovereign, He reigns in us. When we are faithful to do this even the desires of our hearts will be ours.

The way in which we interact with everything in our lives changes, through the prompting of the Holy Spirit. When we realize that God has led us to this time and place in our lives, everything is viewed as belonging to Him, and has been placed there for a reason. All the experiences of love and loss we have known have sculpted us into the person God has called, met, and is transforming to serve Him. All the trials and tests have strengthened us for the coming works. All the times we have fallen short and sinned, and yet have returned has strengthened our resolve to love and serve Him who loved us first.

When we begin to see those around us through the eyes of our God, we begin to see them for their real worth and the perfect love He has for them. They are people so loved by God that He was willing to send His son to suffer and die to heal and redeem them. They are no longer just a spouse we have married; they are God's blessing and partners He has given to share our lives. They are no longer just our pesky neighbors; they are potential brothers and sisters in Christ and people for which Christ died. They are no longer just bosses, or co-workers; they are potentially fellow saints bound for heaven. They are no longer just people we share a pew

35   Romans 5:8
36   Matthew 6:33

24

with at church; they are fellow parts of Christ's body and serve a valuable function to keep that body well. They are no longer just disadvantaged people in our cities; they are Christ Himself who asks for food or drink. God's eyes shine with deep compassion and love, and if we look through these eyes no one will seem unimportant again.

As with the ocean we need to dive into our relationship with God. Wading is good for shore birds, but not for those who seek God. He will only reveal Himself to those who risk complete emersion. Even though we can not use our physical senses to experience Him, we can "see" Him through our Christian family. We can "feel" His love for us and others. We can "hear" His call to the world. God makes Himself available to completely experience if we are truly willing and wait upon His timing. Again, time spent diligently seeking Him is the essence of experiencing Him and His amazing grace and love.

Once we have begun to experience God's love, we will be unable to respond to others without that love. We will begin to truly love everyone and desire the absolute best for them. That of course would be for them to become convicted of their sin and turn to Jesus Christ as their savior, lord, and king, and to join His body of believers. They would then receive the hope, joy, and peace that He supplies, as they realize God's plan for their lives.

STEWARDSHIP

The world around us is a glorious creation. Once we understand our role in the stewardship of it, our response to living in its midst changes. Stewardship is the proper and wise use of all God has given. In regards to the earth's resources, it means neither the abuse, nor the abandonment of the natural world God has given, but to wisely use its resources for the glory of God and benefit of all. When we look upon the world around us as our garden to attend to, we are not so quick to carelessly throw garbage out of the car window. We are not so quick to abuse the use of harmful chemicals. We carefully manage the farm land as well as the forests, and all the animals therein. We should be quick to promote the kind of care that produces bountiful harvests for today, and will insure fertile lands for the harvests of tomorrow.

As we are being transformed our social and cultural views will also change. With stewardship of our society, we become aware of the tendency to drift from the traditional morals and values of our heritage. In a world of sin it is also likely that justice gets overlooked. God would have us be steadfast to secure the rights and freedoms of all through our judicial system so that the weak and poor do not get overlooked or abused.

It is natural for us to resist change. Change almost always involves risk and some amount of fear. If fact the only change we look forward to is in the exchange of money! However, change is the essential ingredient for the life of hope and spirituality we aspire to achieve. Great things often come through risk and sacrifice, and are always worth the effort. Therefore, prepare to change.

POINTS TO PONDER

1. How would being a "new creation" affect me?

2. What change needs to take place in my life?

3. Do I really want change in my life?

4.

PREPARE TO RELATE!

The world is a huge, hostile place. It is full of fallen humans, and under the curse the fall brought. It is also the domain of Satin and his evil forces who seek to destroy us. God created us to be in a close, loving relationship with Him and He intended to be the source for all our needs. He knew that without Him we are weak and vulnerable. God created us to rely on Him while in a union of love and obedience. In our arrogance we rejected Him, but because by our nature we are a communal group and substitute our reliance designed for Him, to others. We find that on our own we have very little ability or strength to be self-sufficient. We search for means to find love, security, and acceptance by forming alliances, as a result of this strong motivating factor to seek others. Having common ground with someone with whom we can form a bond is the basis for forming a relationship. Yet we long for more than just affection or friendship, we unknowingly desire that supernatural love that only God offers and created us to share. We seek approval to be not only wanted by someone, but also needed and loved. Having worth and purpose in our lives drives us to seek out close affiliations.

By having something in common with others we can relate to them. But the drive to experience God's loves causes us to seek more than just to have a mere companionship with them. We seek a special kinship that is deeper than casual acquaintance. We yearn for someone to bond with who accepts us for who we are, is loyal and consistent, and expects us to respond in like manner. These types of partners are rare, but become prized possessions.

If a relationship is possible by having common aspirations, negative or bad commonality can lead to bonding that lies outside society's acceptable morals and ethics, and God's ordinances. This is evident in the gang culture plaguing our society today. This negative commonality may become the loophole Satan can use to spread his evil of lies and deceit. We so badly want to be needed, loved, and to belong that we align ourselves with anyone who deceives us into believing he cares.

Infatuation with those we respect or who pose as something we aspire to be, can cause us to follow them, regardless of their morals. Incorrectly, we assume that these idols possess everything we desire; security, acceptance, wealth, and a host of adoring fans. These fans accept and support their heroes regardless of their actions and lack of character. But, sports heroes and movie stars suffer the same as all of us. We pull for our teams because we secretly wish to a part of something of which we ourselves are not capable. We watch our favorite movies wishing we could experience the adventures and ideal (but fictional) relationships the characters are immersed in. We join clubs to share the sense of accomplishment and to have fellowship with others. We desperately want to have worth and purpose. We are built that way, but we seem to resist the most important group we can belong to that gives us all we desire. That is the body of Christ, the church.

OUR EARLY BONDS

Generally entering the world into a family brings our first sense of both security and belonging. God has instilled into our nature a special love and affection between parents and children. All too often however, circumstances dictate a less than ideal early life. This leads to innumerable problems as young people grow. Being in the same family does not necessarily mean having a good relationship. No person is sinless. Pride and greed can lead to lies, deceit, and selfishness within families that can prevent us from truly loving and serving one another. Often trust can not be proven to be warranted. Erecting barricades can protect us from hurtful situations in life, but they can insulate and isolate us from others. Fear prevents us from letting our defenses down and sharing the intimate areas of our lives. The lack of truth destroys loyalty, and doubt inhibits surrender to one another. Being born into the fallen human race also means that we are innately prone to evil. To fit into the societal norms, others try to teach and train us to live according to the laws society has established and reach to attain those God ordained. This leads to some amount of rebellion to the authority they wield and to all authoritative figures, including God. Shared rebellion can form the commonality needed to start unhealthy relationships.

As we grow and start to find our independence we search outside our family for these types of partnerships. We strive to exert our own values and "rights", and show our autonomy. We turn to those with whom we can relate. We find them in friendships with schoolmates, fellow members of clubs, or perhaps teammates. Whether we find a "good" or "bad" influence to befriend often depends upon the character we have been developing as we grow. We are seeking someone to trust: Someone to share in our existence without fear of being used or exploited; someone to accept us as we are, and in turn we respond the same way. This is the basis on which we seek a relationship. This is the relationship God invites us to.

Some times poor decisions are made in our choice of people we trust. Too often we align ourselves with others also in rebellion and their lies are believed. In our need for someone to trust we become deceived by their evil or selfish ambition to take advantage of our vulnerabilities. The damage that occurs often results in our reluctance to reach out or trust others who are worthy of our trust. It can become a recurring pattern. A wall built around ourselves serves to give some protection, but can prevent healthy relationships from forming.

Life's tests and trials teach us many lessons, both good and bad. These lessons not only develop character, but also provide a testing ground to see who really loves and cares for us, or is just a "fair weather friend". These lessons can provide the means to live healthfully, or to isolate ourselves in an impenetrable shell. The situations and people we become involved with do not mean that we will automatically become bad, but as the saying goes; "staying in a chicken coop will not make you a chicken, but you will surely smell like one." Bad experiences leave us with a bias through which other relationships will be screened.

BUILDING A RELATIONSHIP

How do we develop a relationship? Whenever a new acquaintance is met, attention is given to actions to try and discern motives and trustworthiness. Interaction is limited to a very superficial level until trust can be developed. Time is spent in safe settings where interactions are shallow. Awareness of the evaluation occurring in meeting someone new may not even be apparent but it takes place regardless. Slowly a conclusion is formed regarding the other's intentions and either a severance or a deepening of the relationship is allowed. The risk of being influenced by the biases we have developed in past encounters is a threat to the development of new ones if we fail to be vigilant.

A relationship is strengthened as we become more familiar with each other by spending time together. Furthering relationships require risking deeper thoughts and feelings, while observing the other's reactions. How our new acquaintances interact with others, and how they face adversities informs us of their honesty and integrity. We inspect their response to our invitation to relationship. No decision as to whether the person is someone we could befriend or someone who does not meet our criteria can be made until adequate time is spent together. The essence here is time spent together. Time spent in communicating is not just verbal. Facial expressions and body language are important in forming views of others and often are more honest. Thus, practices such as internet dating and long distance relationships are risky at best.

A lasting relationship must always be mutually beneficial. So, while we are busy evaluating someone else, we are also being evaluated. This calls for honesty and realism from us. Anything but truth and openness mars any hope of a solid friendship, and admitting mistakes and asking for forgiveness expresses more sincerity than hours of idle chat.

The same holds true for us when we reach an age that we become attracted to the opposite gender. To develop a lasting relationship and perhaps marriage, we seek someone with common hopes and plans for the future. They should have like interests and beliefs to begin a friendship, while developing trust and openness. In the normal course of time shared, romance may begin. The hope for a lasting marriage comes from learning about the real person we are engaging, with no lies, no hidden vices, and no deceitful motives. Again, this is only realized through time spent together. In this sin-filled world there is no shortcut to intimate relationship. Nothing will substitute for time spent together to become more familiar, and to learn to trust one another. Beginning at this point love may start and develop into intimacy.

How do we develop a relationship with God? Up to a point we use many of the same methods. At some point we were introduced to God. All have the need for Him built in from our creation, so at some point after hearing about Him, the choice was made to accept His grace and acknowledge that we did not choose Him, but He chose us to go and produce good fruit.[37] This occurs when He reveals Himself to us and we learn of His justice and incredible mercy. Next we need to decide if God is indeed who He says He is. In learning of Him through the Holy Spirit, we can choose to totally surrender ourselves in a trusting manner that we can't with anyone else. As we spend more and more time with Him in prayer and in His written word, a deeper understanding will follow resulting in a deeper and more loving relationship. Again the essence is time spent together.

Through the works of the Holy Spirit we become convicted of our sinful ways and the evil we have exhibited toward God and others.[38] We acknowledge to God that we have broken His laws and by doing so have sinned. Repentance is the next task. This means to amend our way of living from the evil ways we have lived and begin to live in response to the prompting of the Holy Spirit to emulate Jesus Christ. The Holy Spirit reveals what we truly are, terrible sinners deserving punishment and death. God reveals His undying love displayed in the sacrifice of His own Son for payment of all sin. We accept that He is God and begin to put our faith in Him, accepting Jesus Christ as our Savior, Lord, and King. We are then born again of the spirit and are creatures capable of intimacy with God.

After we have met God and found that His character is trustworthy the similarities pale. God knows us better than we know ourselves, because He created us. He has already chosen us unconditionally, regardless of anything we have done or left undone. He has already chosen us to be part of His family, and partake in the beauty of a close and personal relationship with Him. His loving call to us is answered by our choosing Him and His plan over this mortal one we have been living out.

Like the relationships we develop with others, being completely open and honest with God is required. In reality, God already knows when we are not totally forthright with Him. We can not lie to or deceive God. Therefore, we strive to be totally open and honest with *ourselves*. The posturing and false fronts we erect to promote and protect ourselves from others are hindrances in relating to God. When we come to know and understand ourselves through the God's eyes we can become intensely honest.

The Holy Spirit will reveal God's nature and truths in quiet time spent

---

37   John 15:16
38   John 16:8

in prayer, meditation, and devotions. Setting time aside just to be in the Lord's presence provides the opportunity for insight and growth. God will move our hearts in a direction that produces peace and tranquility of mind that is the by-product of being in His will. He may correct or reprimand us as a father might his children, but God will always prompt us to move in the direction of His will and His love. He may just take us into His tender care and love us, soothing our pains and filling us with hope. He may do any number of things in this quiet time for He is totally sovereign and He knows our wants and needs even before we ask.

A great thing then develops. As we grow into that relationship with God, we begin to take on His character. As we submit to the divine purpose presented to us, the Holy Spirit begins transforming our hearts and minds into the likeness of God exhibited through Jesus Christ. We begin to exude the fruit of the Holy Spirit.[39] These are; love, joy, peace, longsuffering, kindness, goodness, faithfulness, gentleness, and self-control. We put to death the corrupt nature of the flesh. We, on our own, have neither the will nor power to do so. We need the power of the Holy Spirit who lives within us to do the work of this transformation. Remember that the triune God, Father, Son, and Holy Spirit, is a perfect gentleman. God will never arrive uninvited, or force His will upon us. He wants us to choose Him to be ours, and to ask Him for all our needs. As we continue to do this, He will faithfully meet our every need according to His standard and fill us with His very presence.

As our relationship with God grows and our likeness changes, our outlook on everyone else will also undergo an amazing transformation. Tolerance and patience toward others will result from the love that God has for each soul He has created. Fellow brothers and sisters in Christ will become dear to us and being with them, especially in worshiping our God, will become very precious to us.

The way in which we relate to all of creation will change. From the way we look at the surrounding landscape to the way we regard the simple aspects of living will seem more friendly and pleasant. The things that were once burdensome will be pleasurable because we do it not for ourselves, but for God, and His glory. Joy will be found in every task where before there was apathy.

---

39   Galatians 5:22 f

FINDING OUR DESIRE

It is only through our relationship with the triune God that all we yearn for and diligently seek in our lives is found. As we reprioritize our lives by putting God first, and making communing with Him our source, we begin to gain our souls yearning. We are assured of love by surrendering to the source of love. We are confident that our lives have meaning and purpose by uniting with the Architect of our existence. We are accepted by the Father because He sent His Son to die for us. We find absolute security in the One who commands angels to watch over us. And, we are empowered by our divine heritage through Jesus Christ to answer every challenge presented to us.

Not to experience this relationship is to muddle through life tossed and blown by every evil intention of every enemy we encounter. This life of unfulfillment ultimately leads to death, both physical and spiritual. And even more terrible, it will probably result in others following this bad example and being lost for eternity themselves.

Though available to be claimed by all, the relationship we have with God is personal. God has created us very specifically with traits unique to each of us. The way someone may use to commune with God is not necessarily going to work for others. That is why we must seek and attend to God in the way He has exclusively designed for each of us. Knowing about God is not the same as being in a relationship with Him. This is only accomplished be accepting His free gift of salvation through His Son and to have the Holy Spirit living in us.

Our relationship with God is an ongoing process. It starts at the time of our salvation, and continues until we meet Him face to face. The critical aspect is to strive to develop it to an ever deeper level, and never, never give up.

POINTS TO PONDER

1. Is it possible for me to relate to God?

2. What needs to happen in my life in order to facilitate a relationship with Him?

3. Does "relating" to God make me part of His family?

5

PREPARE TO PRAY!

Relationships are only as deep as we choose them to be. If we are unsure of another's character or motives, we refrain from revealing ourselves too deeply until we determined the other to be trustworthy. Deep relationships develop and flourish only when the parties take enough time together to develop trust. Then we can dare to risk revealing ourselves while seeking the other's true nature and character. This entails the breaking down of all facades projected to hide our true selves. It also requires graciously listening without judgment, and being a loyal confidant with everything shared with us. By trial and error, success and failure, we have learned how to relate our entire lives.

Our relationship with God is somewhat different in that we must constantly remember that we are not meeting with our peers. While the need for sharing time remains the same, our approach must be different. God and mankind are on separate levels of existence, we are finite and He is infinite. We are matter while He is spirit. We are sinful and corrupt and He is pure and holy. We see only very limitedly and He sees and knows everything. In spite of these differences, He created us in His image to be able to relate closely with Him, and His love for us is so great that He not only allows communion with Him, He deeply desires it.

WHAT IS PRAYER?

In our Christian experience we call time spent together with God prayer. To understand what prayer is, let's first look at what it isn't. Prayer is not a shopping list of things we want. Prayer is not just a last minute S O S when we are in trouble. Prayer is not a compilation of meaningless words designed to make us feel religious. And finally, prayer is certainly not a method for manipulating God to change His mind, or do our bidding. Unfortunately, prayer is often seen as these. In our petitions, God uses prayer not to change things or circumstances as much as He does to change people, including us. Prayer is not overcoming God's reluctance to answer as much as it is reaching for His loving willingness to help.

The English translation of the word prayer most generally is "asking for our needs". This is very shallow compared to the Hebrew word for prayer. That word is "tephilah" which means "to judge oneself." Judging oneself is a very difficult task. We can not hide from ourselves, but we rationalize or deceive ourselves so we do not have to expose the wretched beings we truly are. Unrealistic standards are heaped upon us from birth by parents and society, and we strive in vain to meet them. We build walls of delusion around ourselves to protect us from being judged by anyone, especially God. Every attempt used to fool others is worthless when they have a discerning spirit. In meeting God, He demands that we strip ourselves bare to analyze and judge the way we measure up to *His standards*. We are sure to fail, bringing us to the acknowledgment of our sin and true repentance which provides the means by which humility is born and takes root in our souls. Humility leads to the proper alignment with God, and speeds us on our way toward an eternal relationship with Him. Humility is the starting point for spiritual growth and relationship with God.

The Greek word for prayer is "proseuche". It is derived from two Greek words. The first is "pros" which means advantageous for, but also denotes direction, as in moving toward. The second is "euchomai" which implies wish, or earnest desire. Whether we are aware of it or not, we have a deep desire for love and security beyond that which is attainable in the secular world, as we aspire to rise above mediocrity to have meaning and purpose in living. When we trust in God, we look to Him for favor and plead for His grace to benefit our being. We look toward Him with earnest desire for all that would be advantageous to have in order to lead a fulfilled life.

Prayer is always communication, verbal or nonverbal - a link to the Divine. Time spent in prayer includes the special instances of closeness with our attention being exclusively focused on God. It also includes the awareness of God we experience in every minute of our day. As we become increasingly mature in our Christian walk, everything we think, feel, and seek is communicated through prayer. We express our needs, hopes, fears, frustrations, joy, sorrow, and regrets for ourselves and others to our attentive Father. We also offer our praise, worship, love, adoration, and thanksgiving to the only One who truly desires us to succeed in becoming complete in His plan for us.

Scripture reading, meditation, and prayer give us the time needed to listen to and reflect on who God is and what He desires for us. Application of this knowledge to further His kingdom becomes the natural next step. This brings us to the place where we finally see Him in wonder and awe, and allows us to progress into becoming more and more like Him. Prayer is always a dialog, never a monolog. God always answers faithful prayer even if the answer is no or wait for the correct time. Even His silence is an answer and can reveal His plan for us to grow through the trials we face. When He seems slow to answer, we can still be in His presence to try and fathom His greatness, with worship and praise.

God answers prayers in several ways. He may grant our requests immediately, or He may reveal that the timing is wrong. He may say no to requests or respond by His silence. How can we question God's reason or timing for His answers? He knows what we need long before we ask, and how unanswered prayer can protect or promote our growth. We must simply trust in the eternal love He has for us and have faith that He is in control.

From the moment we accept Jesus Christ as our Savior until the moment death casts its shadow over us we commune with God in prayer. We are called to renounce our wicked ways of living and receive Jesus through Prayer. We turn for solace to Him in our time of weariness and grief through prayer. We attain our position in His Grand Plan through prayer. We seek guidance and power to perform all the actions of our life, knowing nothing of value is accomplished but through prayer. We are inspired by the Holy Spirit for how and what to be prayed for, as well as having our prayers refined and perfected through the Great Mediator through sincere prayer. And, we can best emulate Jesus in fellowship with the Heavenly Father through prayer. Nothing to further the Kingdom of God can transpire without prayer.

THE LORD'S PRAYER

Verbal prayer should follow the example set forth to us by Jesus Christ in the Scriptures. It should include; praise and adoration, a desire that God's plan come to fruition and that His will be accomplished in His creation on earth as it is in Heaven, petitions to Him for our daily sustenance, a confession of sin and seeking forgiveness, giving an acknowledgement of our willingness to forgive in kind, and a desire to be led and protected from ourselves and the evil in the world. This is of course known as the Lord's Prayer. Its beauty is that its simplicity speaks to both the newest Christian as well as the more mature, and reveals God's heart for His creation.

Prayer in our early Christian walk is usually dominated by verbal petitions. We ask for the things we know we need (and sometimes what we just want) as well as for the things God knows we need. We tend to be a bit on the selfish side and do nearly all the talking with little, if any, listening. This is normal because we are accustomed to being in our fallen human nature, seeking to further our own interests. Our inherent greed causes us to seek personal gain, even at the expense of doing what is right. Pride proclaims that we know what our needs are and expects our new loving God to bless us with them. Because God is a loving God, He often does not give us our wishes. God does not allow us to settle for less than He has for us, and He knows how greed and pride move us from being reliant on Him. He knows our full potential, and desires us to grow in wisdom, stature, and in favor with Him. As a father does not give to his young child everything he asks for, so our heavenly Father, for our own good and growth, does not grant our every wish.

DEEPER PRAYERS

As we grow and learn, our prayers begin to also grow in depth. Deepening humility allows us to realize our sinful nature, ask forgiveness, and seek strength to choose His ways rather than pursue our own. The Holy Spirit inspires us to repent of our continuing sin and accept Jesus Christ as our Lord, Savior, and King, surrendering all for Him to govern. The Holy Spirit also moves us to yearn for the perfection of Jesus, as He is our example. The Holy Spirit puts God and ourselves into proper prospective, He as Creator and we as His creation. He also fills us with awe and wonder and inspires praise with thanksgiving. Our deepening faith moves us away from being totally self-centered, and directs us to be

Christ centered, having concern for God's people and creation, leading us to pray for them.

Communion with God is one objective in reading the Scriptures and meditating. Reading and contemplating God's word is one of the primary ways in which God reveals Himself to His people. We should always expect and seek to find God and His plan throughout the Bible. As He has said: knock and keep on knocking, and the door will be opened. Seek and keep on seeking and you will find. Ask and keep on asking and it will be given.[40] God is always faithful to those who earnestly seek Him.

At those times when we face severe difficulties or when our minds fail in knowing how to pray, God Himself gives the words or utterances through his Holy Spirit.[41] We may never know the words used, or thoughts expressed when we pray like this, but we have faith that God is always mindful of us and merciful to us. We may never know the result of those prayers, but we can rest in the fact that being obedient to His command puts us in proper alignment to receive all the blessings and promises He has made available.

TYPES OF PRAYER

There are several types of verbal prayers. There is "petition", which is asking for our requests of God. There is also "supplication" which is the pleaful request for God's intervening assistance. Also we have "beseeching" which is the earnest insistence for a favorable answer from God. These prayers are somewhat similar but differ by the depth and intensity of need.

Other prayers include "adoration", which is showing the love and affection we have toward the One who made us and reconciled us back to Him. This also entails having the proper awe and respect for God, as well as having a "fear" for the ultimate power of His righteous wrath for all who deny Him. In similar fashion there is prayer of "thanksgiving". We show our deep gratitude for all the blessings God has richly showered upon us, from having life to the grace bestowed upon us enabling us to become His children, and everything in between. Everything we are and have are blessings from His hand. Included here is also "communion". Spending time just enjoying closeness is some of the deepest prayer possible. Being

---

40   Matthew 7:7
41   Romans 8:26

still in adoring silence brings great pleasure to our heavenly Father, for it is at that time we finally become that for which we were created.

God is so holy that sin can not be in His presence. Our sins are a stain on us, and prevent our prayers from reaching God's ears. While we are tainted with sin He denies access to Himself. The word sin often is blanketed over three types of our failings. In Greek there are ten words indicating various aspects of "sin". The most commonly used means "misses the mark" or "accepting less than God's best for us". This entails ignorance of the ordinances of God and therefore violating them in both actions taken and those omitted. Iniquity denotes knowledge of statutes but straying from the narrow path by lacking the self-control to choose correctly. Transgression is open rebellion, knowing but refusing to obey God's ordinances. Christ died to atone for all these sins if we are faithful to confess them, plead His blood to wash us clean, and amend our living to be within God's intentions. Following His means of restoration and salvation restores our access to God and then He will hear us. This should be included in prayer. God knows what sins we are guilty of, and He wants us to acknowledge them before Him and agree that what we have done is wrong, thus continuing our journey toward Him. Confession and repentance are essential to prayer. As we have been taught by Jesus in the "Lord's Prayer", we are forgiven in only when we are willing to forgive others. If we are hard-hearted toward others and are unwilling to forgive them by holding on to our anger, God, can not forgive us in our obstinacy, thereby preventing us from shedding the guilt of our sin, which causes prayer to go unanswered.

As we begin to assume our new identity in God, and begin to love as He does we begin to have a burden to pray for other people and circumstances as He leads. Prayer for family and close friends is normal for all, but at God's leading we may pray for people and events of which we have no knowledge. Some are specially gifted and sensitive to the needs of others which God brings to mind, and intersession (standing in the gap) is their primary personal ministry. Everyone is called to participate in intersession at some level.

God may communicate in response in any number of ways. He may reply directly to us through the Holy Spirit with His "still, small voice". God may respond as we read His word in the scriptures, or through a member of our family, friends, or clergy. God may send visions or dreams to lead us to His meaning. And, God may choose to be silent now and respond at the later, appropriate time. We need to be sure we never limit God by denying the way He sovereignly reveals knowledge or hold Him to our time table. Our desire should be to become mature and submitted enough to know God's mind and will. In other words we strive to surrender ourselves to allow the Holy Spirit to change us into the likeness of Jesus, being in God as He was. If we do, we become empowered to use authoritative prayer. This is what Jesus meant in the Bible when He said "whenever two of you agree on earth concerning anything that they ask, it will be done for them by My Father in heaven."[42] Also Jesus said, "And I will do whatever you ask in my name, so that the Son may bring glory to the Father."[43] When two or more gather in Jesus' name, He has promised to be there and share His authority with them when they pray by the inspiration of the Holy Spirit. Through this inspiration of the Holy Spirit we are directed toward the purpose and will of God. After we have discerned His will and purpose, we then pray for what He desires. He will always answer this prayer, in His timing and perfect manner.

IN THE NAME OF JESUS

Some seem to think that praying in the name of Jesus is a magic formula for manipulating God to do our bidding. Far indeed from the truth this is! When we use the name of Jesus in prayer we are reaffirming the fact that we are part of His earthly body of believers, those who have confessed and repented their sin, and have given Him dominion over them. Through all of this we take our place with Him in His death and glorious ascension. Jesus name reminds us to remain humble, keeps in focus what we should be about, and causes our prayers to be heard in heaven.

Although seldom use in today's vernacular, we are familiar with old stories or movies where a policeman would say, "stop in the name of the law", or a courier would say "I come in the name of the king". When this was heard, it was understood that that person had the delegated authority of the delegator, whether it was the sheriff or the king. This is the authority that was given to Jesus. Many acknowledged this as evident in Jesus' triumphant entry into Jerusalem. They shouted "Hosanna to the Son of David! Blessed is He that comes *in the name* of the Lord!" They understood that the miracles He preformed, and the wisdom used to teach came with the authority of God.

When we are in Jesus as He was in the Father, we have access to this

---

42   Matthew 18:19
43   John 14:13 NIV

same authority. As Jesus said "I tell you the truth, anyone who has faith in me will do what I have been doing. He will do even greater things than these, because I am going to the Father."[44] When we are in the will of God, authoritative prayer will result in the healing, liberation, and reclaiming of souls to the glory of the Father. All the miracles in the Bible are within the power of those who are inspired to pray for them to come to fruition.

Jesus said, "Have faith in God. I tell you the truth, if anyone says to this mountain, 'go throw yourself into the sea,' and does not doubt in his heart but believes that what he says will happen, it will be done for him. Therefore I tell you, whatever you ask for in prayer, believe that you have received it, and it will be yours."[45] Obviously Jesus shows that faith is vital to prayer. We do not simply hope for answers, we believe even as we are praying that they are already answered. What then do we have faith in? It is not *what* we have faith in; it is *whom* we have faith in. We believe that God, Father, Son, and Holy Spirit is what He says He is. This is where we put our faith. When we believe this, what He has promised is also true. Faith is a decision we must make. But God grants us deeper faith when we ask for it through prayer.

TRAITS NEEDED FOR PRAYER

Faith always grows as we learn from experience. As young children we may have been frightened when our fathers swung us around. As we experienced his strong loving arms we began to have faith that he was in control and that he would never harm us. After several times of being swung we became confident that we were safe and began enjoying the loving playfulness he was showing. The more we apply faith, the deeper it becomes.

Prayers for what we desire need to be specific. When we go to a doctor for some ailment what does he do? He begins a relentless series of questions, each narrowing down the specific time, place, and acuteness of various symptoms. In other words he demands that we be very specific so he may diagnose and proscribe treatment. Could he help us if we are not honest and very specific? Generally we have an understanding of the need we have, but if we don't, we must inquire about our need and believe that the Holy Spirit will inspire us to correctly ask or pray Himself on our behalf. If we are not specific when we ask, how will we understand when and how a

44   John 14:12 NIV
45   Mark 11:23-24 NIV

prayer is answered? When we are specific in prayer we can better grasp the answer, be it yes, no, or later.

We must always pray earnestly. Talking to the Creator of the universe is not to be taken lightly. Even when our prayers are gravely serious, we can make no demands of Him. All we can do is request and have faith that God in His infinite wisdom, love, and grace will meet our needs, both to satisfy us, and to fulfill His purpose. When we have not seen an answer we should persevere in our requests. The apostle Paul asked and was turned down three times in his request to be healed from his "thorn in the flesh". Yet, wisdom is often found in an unanswered prayer and in the assurance that His grace is sufficient.

To expect our prayer to be answered, we must be obedient. As youngsters, did we expect our parents to grant our wishes if we were rebellious and disobedient? Did we hope to get a good grade in school if we did not listen to the teacher or her instructions? The answer is of course no. If we are disobedient to God we are not in any position for Him to ever hear our prayer let alone having our prayers answered. To be in Christ, we must emulate Him. That is, do as He did by pray unceasingly and be totally obedient to the will of God the Father.

Part of the obedience we show to the Father is the complete self-sacrificing of all we are, including fasting. We are told that fasting should be a normal part of our prayer lives. Jesus said "When you fast, do not look somber as the hypocrites do, for they disfigure their faces to show men they are fasting. I tell you the truth; they have received their reward in full. But when you fast, put oil on your head and wash your face, so that it will not be obvious to men that you are fasting, but only to your Father, who is unseen; and your Father, who sees what is done in secret, will reward you".[46] He said *when* you fast, not *if* you fast, thereby commanding us to do so.

Fasting is the choice to give up the first right God gave to Adam, to be a blessing for him and Eve. In the creation story we read. "The Lord God took the man and put him in the Garden of Eden to work it and take care of it. And the Lord God commanded the man, 'You are free to eat from any tree in the garden; but you must not eat from the tree of the knowledge of good and evil, for when you eat of it you will surely die.' "[47] The satisfaction of eating from the fruit of the Garden of Eden was the first noted right given to man. When we fast we are not denying God's

46   Matthew 6:16-18 NIV
47   Genesis 2:15-17

blessings upon us, we willingly abstain from the self satisfaction of eating. We deny our wants to show our submission to God. This fasting is done in conjunction with prayer and meditation. When we do this to honor our Creator, our petitions become more focused and pleasing to Him.

God does not need our prayers. He will still be God whether or not we pray to Him. But, He passionately desires our prayers. Nothing we do or say can change God's will or purpose, but it changes us! That is His ultimate goal for us, to ever change into a closer likeness of Jesus Christ. We learn humility when we acknowledge His glory and learn our inadequacies, but His power can best be displayed by our meekness. God is glorified when we realize our absolute need for Him and His bountiful goodness. God is well pleased with us when we finally learn to love others and creation enough to ask His blessing upon them. One of the main purposes of prayer is love; to love God, to love others, and to love of all His creation.

Prayer is not an obligation, it is a privilege. To share in the closeness of open dialog with God is beyond our wildest dreams, for it forms our faith, hope, and love. It is a window into life as it was intended, and a glimpse into the glorious hereafter.

POINTS TO PONDER

1. If God knows everything what is the point of praying?

2. If God is in full control and His will shall be done, how can prayer change things?

3. Has your prayer life been limited to just talking to God? What other means can you use to communicate with Him?

6

PREPARE TO BE FOOLISH!

The mind and wisdom of God are incomprehensible to human understanding. The vast wealth of knowledge required to plan the least of God's creation overwhelms the most intelligent person if he has the courage and insight to admit it. This is to be expected. Can a book have a story line other that that which the author inserted into it? Can a plan be more detailed than the planner who designs it? The answer is, of course, no. Finite humans can only do what our Creator has given us to do. Progress can only advance as far as knowledge given and some things will remain a mystery until we reach heaven. Striving, but not fully achieving, is the result of our fall from grace even though God encourages us, by His power, to achieve all He has prepared for us.

Since the creation and subsequent fall of mankind, this hasn't been sufficient for us. We seek to be self-sufficient and independent, totally autonomous. The forces of evil and our own selfish desires have taught us that which makes us prosperous and "successful." Success and failure as defined by the world have deceived us into basing our opinions on its unreliable data. After generations of practicing these traits, they become the norm, and are accepted as the "right" way to live and become accomplished in the eyes of the world. This then becomes the knowledge of the world that brings with it worldly success, underachieving, or even worse, failure. As mankind has progressed in the study of God's creation and gained some understanding of its complexity, we have become very arrogant, proclaiming that we have the wisdom needed to lead a successful life. All these rules and manmade systems are grievously wrong when compared to God's plan. God has revealed that which is essential for mankind to be successful and fulfilled. The Bible is filled with knowledge of the Creator's plan for His highest creation. Often this wisdom is paradoxical and brings scorn and public contempt, but God is always faithful to bless those who trust and obey Him. After all, the One who creates us knows the means by which we can find meaning and contentment. God's wisdom and plan is very different from that of the astute and "learned" leaders of man. To them God's way is foolishness and those who follow His laws are also "foolish" and are doomed to failure.

OLD TESTAMENT "FOOLISHNESS"

One of the earliest examples of "foolishness" in the Bible is the story of Noah.[48] We can only imagine a man over 500 years old, building a boat 450 feet long with no body of water nearby to use it. This vessel was so large that no means of transport was available to move it. We can hear the jeers and insults thrown upon this man of God, especially since Noah was the only "good" man alive. Not only did he spend many years and all the labor needed to complete such an undertaking, but it took a considerable amount of resources also. Then to top everything off, Noah began to gather all the animals God required him to save from the coming flood. The hoots must have been deafening to Noah. Yet all the laughter and criticism became silent when the torrential rains began to fall. The worldly wisdom of that age was not sufficient to save even one of those wicked people. We are all glad that Noah chose to be "foolish."

The next example of "foolishness" in the Bible is Abraham.[49] Abraham was a man who left a good life of considerable means and family in an established region to head toward some unknown land which God had promised him. At the age of 100 years he still believed God's promise that he would become a father to a son, and patriarch of many nations. After his son was finally born, he was "foolish" enough to offer that only son to God as a sacrifice. To the wisdom of the world it seems Abraham was foolish his entire life. Yet there are few accounts of men throughout history that have become more rich or powerful than Abraham. His descendents

---

48   Genesis 6:9ff
49   Genesis 12:1ff

include many nations, and all who believe in God are his spiritual children. Again, how thankful we are that through his faith this man chose to be "foolish."

The Old Testament is full of stories of devout people who choose God's "foolishness" over the normal system or wisdom of the world. Many of God's miracles look foolish to the world and are unfathomable. But that is God's way. We are to be God's "holy" people. One definition of the word holy is described as being "set above for special purpose". It means having the faith to believe and obey all that God in His wisdom asks of us even at the risk of looking foolish to the world.

"FOOLISHNESS" OF CHRIST

Jesus Christ's teachings in the New Testament further expound the difference between God's wisdom and the wisdom of the world. Jesus illustrated such "foolishness" in the Sermon on the Mount.[50] He said:

"Blessed are the poor in spirit: for theirs is the kingdom of heaven." This means that those who examine and find themselves lacking in spirit need to come with the attitude and position of a beggar and literally beg for the divine essence and knowledge to be instilled into them so that the Kingdom and its King may have entrance into them. The awareness of reliance on God to furnish His knowledge brings deepening humility to the poor in spirit and acceptance as a child of God. To the world acknowledging the lack of anything is looked at as a sign of weakness, a flaw that others might use to their advantage. But this is the condition that allows God to intervene on our behalf and bring His countenance upon us.

"Blessed are those who mourn: for they shall be comforted." Only those who love can truly mourn the deceased, and only those who love with the love of Jesus can mourn the lost. Every time we fall short of God's plan and blessings for us we suffer. We lament the loss of "what could be" when we settle for "what is". We also suffer and morn for close friends who experience grief and pain. This is caused by having God's loving spirit as then we are akin to the His nature of love. He begins to fill the emptiness He knows we suffer through with the Holy Spirit and those in His body. We welcome His comforting presence. The world sees mourning as a means of gaining, either financially from inheritance, or the pity and

---

50   Matthew 5:1-12KJV

sympathy of others. The world seeks only to gain from, but not comfort others who grieve.

"Blessed are the meek: for they shall inherit the earth." Meekness is humility and gentleness. All too often this is look at as a lack of motivation or competency. In the world's view the aggressive "go-getters" are the leaders that show success in their living. These proud and arrogant people will never submit to anyone, not even God. But, being humble is not weakness. It is an acknowledgement of God's authority and power living within us which gives confidence and abilities without needing to promote our own cause. Being gentle is another way of not lauding ourselves over others by being aggressive and hurtful. This trait also gives us the ability to acknowledge our deficiencies and shortcomings and allows the Holy Spirit to assist in supplementing and changing them. Meekness is the attribute of those who will receive the blessings and are joint heirs of the heavenly kingdom.

"Blessed are they that hunger and thirst after righteousness: for they will be filled." Imagine putting forth time and energy to seek what is right and true rather than what is merely profitable. We all have had the sensations of being hungry and thirsty. We think of little else until that feeling is satisfied. This hunger and thirst mentioned here is insatiable, leaving little contentment while we are being fed. We continually seek and strive to fill the void that a lack of righteousness causes. The world says righteousness is not an item that can be listed on a balance sheet and provides no way to wealth and fame, so it is useless. Reprioritizing is what we hold important, putting God and His desire for us before all our goals, hopes or plans. God has said that the best way to continue our relationship with Him is to become like Him, righteous and holy people. This can only happen as we accept the righteousness imparted to us from Christ. He will then satisfy us fully.

"Blessed are the merciful: for they shall obtain mercy." The world proclaims; to the victor goes the spoils. Also, all is fair in love and war. All too often life is seen as an all or none proposition. If we do not get it all we may get nothing. We seek to gain success at the expense of others, and are seldom merciful in our approach. We covet what we see and will do anything to satisfy our desires. To be merciful is a weakness which allows the competition to win. Forgetting past transgressions and debts is something the world also scorns. We are all less than perfect. If we ever hope to be forgiven, and have compassion shown to us, we must forgive and show compassion to all others as well. We will be judged by our own standard of being merciful.

At times we have all found ourselves in a position of despair and misery in the circumstances of life. At these times we look lovingly toward anyone who will have mercy upon us and help us. This has already been done in that "For God so loved the world that he gave his one and only Son, that whoever believes in him shall not perish but have eternal life"[51] Can we do less for others?

"Blessed are the pure in heart: for they shall see God." "We all have our faults" is the common excuse of the world. "Everybody cheats, lies, and steals." "There is no way for us to be pure when surrounded by so many wicked people." That is true to their way of thinking. The only way we can become pure is to be cleansed by the One who shows us our iniquities. He sets the standard for purity and removal of evil from within, and provides the only means for obtaining it. That is the confession of our sins, changing from our wicked ways, and receiving forgiveness through the blood of Jesus Christ. This is the only way we can enter the presence of God and catch a glimpse of His glory, and to begin to take His character as our own. Anything that is not pure cannot be close to God for His glory and power repel it. Purity allows access to the knowledge of God that we may "see" him in our daily walk, and that we will we be able to continue to "see" Him forever.

"Blessed are the peacemakers: for they shall be called the children of God." When love is alive in us and we truly wish the best for all men, we strive to find any method of resolving differences other than violence. This is also true when we try to resolve problems between others. We desire to be harmonious with all men of good character and all in the body of Christ who are His children. We cultivate an environment that allows dignity and peace to flourish. However, there is no way to find peace with evil, since the Devil desires our downfall and destruction. The worldly view cannot distinguish the difference between the two. They believe that conflict leads to conquest, conquest leads to success, and success leads to fulfillment.

The implication of the term children here is the same one used in Biblical times to indicate a child which had the blessing of the father to inherit his patriarchal position. This means that this child would be in control of the estate at the father's passing. We therefore have been given the position of power and prominence to do God's will in His family as we live out lives as peacemakers.

---

51   John 3:16 NIV

"Blessed are the persecuted for righteousness' sake: for theirs is the kingdom of heaven." To endure persecution is a daunting task. To be continually sought by those wishing to do us harm temps us into giving in and surrendering our beliefs, or retaliate as the world would. We who are in Christ should expect to endure persecution. After all, He was sinless and completely faultless and He was hated and persecuted even to His death. Jesus endured and overcame those who sought Him harm. Because of this, God gave Him authority and dominion over all creation as King. We too then become joint heirs with Jesus in the heavenly kingdom if we endure as He did, both now as He reigns in us, and in the world to come. The world says that the effort required would not be worth the potential benefit, or this couldn't possibly be true, so just be vengeful. The world argues that compromise and negotiations are far more profitable than enduring anything as unpleasant as this.

"Blessed are you, when men shall revile you, and persecute you, and shall say all manner of evil against you falsely, for my sake." The Hope of the resurrection that Jesus taught is the means by which we endure these hardships. The short term discomfort we experience is nothing compared to the eternal reward in which we will partake. To overcome, the power and assurance given by the Holy Spirit is required. God promised an outpouring of the Holy Spirit to all who ask for it. Those of the world try to befriend anyone who may be of use. They are willing to compromise their morals and beliefs to be popular. This closeness is needed in order to be in the position to use or manipulate others. Besides, defending against such attacks is just not worth it. "Let's just get along", is what is heard, but their mind adds, "So you can be of some benefit to me".

"Rejoice and be exceeding glad: for great is our reward in heaven: for so persecuted they the prophets which were before you." Only those who have faith in Jesus could ever rejoice in being the object of slander and scorn. Being scorned as Jesus assures us that we are doing His bidding and are on the pathway to glory with Him. We live in the surety that nothing suffered could separate us from His love or dim the eternal glory we shall witness after this mortal life is through. The world says this is foolishness, for we must be doing something wrong to be so despised.

The Beatitudes were the starting point of teaching for Christ's disciples. These lessons were and are intended not for just believers, but for those who strive to become closer to Him by being disciples. Disciples are those who continue to be taught about and by the triune God. Many can and will believe in Jesus Christ, but only those who continually seek and learn are disciples. Another definition of discipleship is to teach, lead, and mentor others up to the level we have reached.

The promises of the blessed; "for theirs is the kingdom of heaven," "for they shall be comforted," "for they shall inherit the earth," etc. are not for causal believers. Christ was setting the ground work for teaching a group of leaders the path to be partakers in a fulfilled life, evangelizing others to take up His cause, and bring the kingdom of heaven to earth.

"FOOLISH" LOVE

Later during that same teaching Jesus again shocked the multitude with more "foolishness." He had the audacity to say that we should not only love our neighbors, but also our enemies. We are to "do good to those that hate you," and "pray for those who spitefully use you and persecute you." Wow! Can you imagine the scoffing and ridicule thrown at Jesus at that statement? Can you imagine how perplexing these words to all who were present? The history of man before this revolved around conquest and strife of nation against nation, and man against man. Hating and reviling one another was standard fare. Love was reserved for a close and intimate group that one could trust. Love was not for just anyone, and surly not for enemies.

The love familiar to the world before Christ was far from the love of God of which Jesus was speaking. After the fall of mankind, we were alienated from God, and we forgot about the love of our Creator. Instead, we substituted that which made us feel good, calling it love, for the essence of God's nature, Divine Love. What we considered love was the enjoyment and pleasure received from a spouse and family, or a close friend, or any other worldly thing. The world's system taught us to believe in an artificial love, which leaves us unsatisfied and unfulfilled. This is the love that those who heard Jesus thought He meant. The world that has never experienced God's love can never accept this truth, and sees it and those who believe it as "foolish."

Jesus then had the nerve to tell us not to worry about our lives, or what we will eat and what we will drink. Sustenance and shelter were among the first concerns of man since he was expelled from his original home in the garden. The cursed earth bore thorns and thistles on its own, and only through the sweat of our brow could we receive nutrition from the earth.[52] Jesus was proclaiming the coming of a new promise of relationship with

52   See Genesis 3

God. Man again had the opportunity to know and receive God's love. To be one of those who hope for a relationship with God we had to rely on God's providence to supply our needs. In the world of sinful man, self-reliance is the only way to secure everything sought for. They feel that even if God will supply their needs, He will not supply the amount they seek, the type they desire, or do it within their time frame. So to them this is a futile gesture and not worth the effort to attempt.

There are many more paradoxes in Scripture dealing with man. For example: Those who will be greatest in the Kingdom of God must come with the honesty, openness, and innocence of a child.[53] Those who are first will be last, and those who are last will be first.[54] He who would be greatest in the Kingdom of God must be the servant of all[55] just as Jesus displayed. And those who are exalted will be humbled, and those who are humble will be exalted.[56] All these examples are purely nonsense and foolishness to the world, but they are God's way.

Perhaps the greatest paradox is the fact that God has decreed that whoever seeks to save his life will lose it, and whoever gives his life will save it.[57] Whoever heard of such "foolishness?" If we give the very thing that we all strive to embrace and embellish, who can ever be happy or fulfilled? What is the purpose of life then? Why do we struggle all the days of our lives if it is for naught? This supposes that we own ourselves. It goes back to the fall when the sovereignty of our Creator was ignored. He created us for His purpose and He has the right to expect us to fulfill that purpose. This does not presume that God is harsh, for He knows that which will fulfill our deepest needs and wants, but loves us enough to allow us to choose something less.

THE GREAT PARADOX

God Himself is paradoxical: He is one God in three parts; Separate but equal. Having different forms but with the same essence. United in a unique relationship that defies all human logic and understanding. God loved man so much that He willingly became human to suffer and experience death to atone for all our sins and transgressions even while mankind was rebellious by hating and reviling Him. In spite of this God

53   Matthew 18:3
54   Matthew 20:16
55   Mark 10:43-45
56   Matthew 23:12
57   Mark 8:35

demonstrated His love for us that while we were still sinners, Christ died for us.[58] Would anyone in great earthly power and position do that? Not in a million years.

Many who consider themselves Christian fail to see the great paradox of God. We as weak, imperfect creatures can never do anything to atone for our manifest sin, but we hope that if we do good works we can be forgiven. How terrible to think God is that shallow. How insulting to think that He could be bought off. His justice could never allow sin to go unpunished. His deep love shows His capacity for emotion, which makes His anger equally great. His wonderful love and mercy is counterpart to His mighty wrath. He alone has provided the means for all who believe to be forgiven, and that way is through the death and resurrection of Jesus Christ. This greatest of gifts cannot be purchased at any price. It is given freely to us as part of His amazing Grace. This is so simple but so many say it is utter foolishness.

So how is it then that the wisest and most powerful people miss these truths while others hold them so dear? What have we done to have these truths plant themselves into our hearts and lives to become part of us? The answer is humility and God's grace. We have done an assessment of who we are and by God's revelation have determined that we are not the source of wisdom and power. We have fallen far short of the standard God has set for us and are sinful, wicked beings. Having sought and found Him Who is our source, and we have assumed our position as created and not Creator. God has sent His Holy Spirit into us to give us discerning and wisdom from above. We have lowered our esteem and raised His to the proper level. For from humility comes truth. From truth comes faith. From faith comes the ability to become sons of God. And being sons of God gives us the ability to have the courage and conviction to be "foolish" for God.

POINTS TO PONDER

1. What does the Bible mean when it speaks about being a fool for Christ?

2. Am I willing to be thought foolish for Jesus' sake?

3. In what way would being foolish for Christ play out in my life?

---

58   Romans 5:8

7

PREPARE TO BE FRUITFUL!

Jesus said that we are not to judge unto condemnation, but we are to critique everyone and recognize His followers by the good fruit they exhibit. Jesus said "By their fruit you will recognize them. Do people pick grapes from thorn bushes, or figs from thistles? Likewise every good tree bears good fruit, and a bad tree bears bad fruit. A good tree can not bear bad fruit, and a bad tree can not bear good fruit. Every tree that does not bear good fruit is cut down and thrown into the fire. Thus by their fruit you will recognize them."[59] Christ's body should not be judgmental, but discerning. Observation of Christ's followers will show the evidence of the Holy Spirit's work which transforms them from the evil beings they are by nature, into new creations, and brings them into their positions in the holy body of Christ's church. Discerning of the character exhibited will reveal whether they live for and gratify the desires of the sinful nature, or live for Jesus Christ through the Holy Spirit.

The scripture lists the acts of the sinful nature as: "sexual immorality, impurity, sensuality, idolatry and witchcraft, hatred, discord, jealousy, fits of rage, selfish ambition, dissentions, factions and envy, drunkenness, carousing, and things like these."[60] These traits are evident in those who live in the natural sinful condition of fallen mankind, and whose lord is Satan. The traits that are evident in those who have denied themselves and

59   Mathew 7:16-20
60   Galatians 5:19-21

taken on a life for Jesus are called the fruit of the Spirit. These Christians live in the blessed hope of all the saints, and exhibit a beautiful difference from those of the world. This fruit is: "love, joy, peace, patience, kindness, goodness, faithfulness, gentleness, and self-control."[61]

WHY FRUIT?

What are the connotations of fruit? When we first think of fruit we think of a delicious healthy and nutritious food. Because of this, fruit is a valuable and marketable commodity sought after by many. The same is true for the fruit of the Spirit, for it holds health giving benefits and blessings, and is essentially valuable for all who display or witness it. Good fruit is only produced on a good, healthy tree. So it is with the fruit of the Spirit; it is produced in one who is spiritually healthy. Fruit trees are tended by farmers who prune and trim them to maximize both the quantity and quality of fruit. Likewise it is with the fruit of the Spirit. We are trimmed and pruned by our Heavenly Gardener that we may produce fruit from His full abundance. One definition of fruit is a seed bearing vessel which is capable of perpetuating its species. The fruit of the Spirit is also capable of reproducing itself in others, bringing unity and love to the whole community. The word fruit, as in the fruit of the Holy Spirit, was well conceived and holds deep meaning for those who choose to see.

THE FRUIT OF THR SPIRIT

Even though there are nine aspects listed as fruit of the Spirit, it is called "fruit" and not fruits. Each segment is intricately connected to other segments and is inseparable from them. All are closely associated and an off shoot of the first one, love. We are not at liberty to choose those we may wish to show, and refuse others. We have little to do with how they present themselves to the world. That is the job of the Holy Spirit. Fruit encompass the total life of the believer when he is in obedience to the leading and transformation of the Holy Spirit. Each trait should be present all the time, and while no segment of the fruit is superior or inferior to the rest, each will manifest itself more fully at various times through our obedience as the need arises, as determined by the Holy Spirit.

---

61   Galatians 5:22-23

LOVE

It is little wonder that love is the first attribute listed. We are told to "Love the Lord your God with all your heart and with all your soul and all your mind." And also "Love your neighbor as yourself."[62] Jesus said that the total of all the law and prophets is summed up in these two commandments. Jesus even said to love your enemies! We obviously are all intended to be creatures of love. The form of love here is the Greek word agape which is translated as the love of God, which is to earnestly desire the absolute best for all, even at the cost of personal sacrifice. It is not just a warm fuzzy feeling or erotic passion, but the desire that the perfection of God would come into being. With love for God and of God, we deeply desire that all He has planned for His creation should come to realization, His creation should give Him the praise, honor, and glory He deserves, and be filled with awe at His greatness. This type of love was expressed by God in many instances in the scriptures, the greatest being His love shown by sending His only begotten Son to us in human form to atone for the sins of the whole world and bring us to the possibility of a relationship with Him. His love was so great for us that "while we were still sinners, Christ died for us".[63] With love for our neighbors we wish for them every good thing that God has planned for their well-being and showing through our actions the intent we have for them.

Jesus gave a "new" commandment to His disciples, "Love one another, as I have loved you, so you must love one another. By this all men will know that you are my disciples, if you love one another."[64] When we become followers of the Lord Jesus Christ, love becomes the natural expression of fellowship through the Holy Spirit. It is not a forced labor on our part, in fact we only need to allow love to flow through us and resist the evil found in our old sinful nature.

To love as God does requires our whole being. It involves allowing our spirit to know God and know that He is drawing us to Himself and to all others. It involves our mind to put into action what we have learned, and our emotions to truly show concern and pleasure with others. Finally, it involves using our bodies to carry forth His decrees and plans. Love is not passive it is active, demanding a new direction to all our relationships by seeing people and situations through the eyes of the One who is love. It is

---

62   Matthew 22:37-40 NIV
63   Romans 5:8 NIV
64   John 13:34-35

no wonder then that love is one of the things that will eternally endure, and is the first on the list of fruit of the Spirit.

JOY

Joy is often hard to associate with the solemn and serious manner in which people react to religion. God is seen in the Old Testament as the giver of laws and judge over those who were guilty, and His wrath was swift and terrible. He was seen as all powerful and all knowing and demanded death as the wages of sin. It took the coming of Jesus Christ to show the truer nature of God. The angel on that blessed morning announced the birth of the Savior by proclaiming "Do not be afraid. I bring you good news of great joy that will be for all the people."[65] God was full of joy upon the completion of creation, and as He looked upon all He had made He said "it is good".[66] After the fall of man He was joyful when righteous men loved and served Him. Jesus also was joyful in life and often attended celebrations and dinners with His friends. He brought man the chance for joy by removing from him the yoke of slavery to sin and death which had kept him bound.

Today joy is often seen as superficial and phony. Often the joy we see is giddiness or at best, a perversion of true joy. We have been so badly beaten about by life in an evil world, that showing true joy is difficult. Nearly everything we hear is negative and is part of Satan's effort to thwart the Spirit's attempt to have creation show joy at God's love and mercy. True joy is seen in a young child on Christmas morning as the family gathers together around the tree to open presents. He feels the anticipation of receiving gifts while being accepted in the safety and warmth of his loving family. At that moment nothing else in the world matters. He knows who he is, where he is, what he is doing, and that he is blessed with belonging. This is also how we should feel upon knowing Jesus as our savior. We anticipate all the blessings from the forgiveness of sins and feel the accepting love and security of our gracious heavenly Father while surrounded in His and now our, family.

As believers in this state of grace, we should be attuned to the beauty and involvement of God in our lives. Every day we should be counting and considering our blessings, for if God ever removed them we would not only be woeful, but would surly die. The awareness of overwhelming wellbeing

65   Luke 2:10
66   Genesis 1:31

with God in control of our lives, and unshakeable confidence in eternal life is cause for great joy. God loves us and has opened the pathway of life to its fullest on Earth and eternal life in heaven. We should approach life full of joy, ever mindful of our blessings and respond from a state of well-being.

This does not mean that our lives will be carefree and painless. Since we are in Jesus we should expect to live the life He did. Often He was filled with joy, but He also experienced rejection, torment, and persecution. Jesus accepted these things graciously and never lost His joy. He knew that He was loved and accepted by His father and that the joy that would follow was far greater than the temporary sufferings He was experiencing then. Simply being loved, redeemed, and sanctified by God is reason to be joyful and to live accordingly.

PEACE

Peace is regarded today as the absence of conflict, tension, or noise. This is not the peace listed in the fruit of the spirit, or the peace given by Jesus to His disciples. If peace was just the absence of an aggravation we would be able to manipulate a situation to unburden ourselves from it and create peace ourselves. The peace in the fruit of the Spirit is not of our own making and is not of this world. It is a gift from God in the realization that He has everything under control and in His special order. It comes as a result of our total submission to God, and being aware and trusting in His promises made to all who remain faithful. This leads us to the wholeness of being that we were created to have.

Jesus told His followers that their lives would be filled with seasons of pleasure, but also seasons of pain and persecution. But, He promised to be with them in every season and never leave them, even to the end of time.[67] This promise gives us a sense of well-being and assurance. If the One who has all authority in heaven and on earth, and deeply loves us is in control, how then could we fear and worry over any circumstance? As long as we are faithful to Him, He will show His faithfulness to us. Approaching life with the confidence that the Lord is in control is like starting a baseball game knowing the outcome before the first pitch. Again this does not mean that we will not suffer disappointment when the road of life takes a sudden, unexpected turn through illness, death, or tragedy, but faith brings us to the place of resolution that He is loving and still in control.

Before we can experience the peace of God, we must find peace with

---

67   Matthew 28:20

God. Peace with God involves being reconnected to Him in the order He established at creation. He is Designer and Creator, and we are the product of His genius. He is the potter and we are the clay He fashions to His delight. Confessing our sins and claiming redemption through Jesus Christ, the means God ordained for man to return to His grace, is the first step to aligning ourselves back to His perfect order. Allowing the transforming work of the Holy Spirit in us is the next step. This is an on going process and brings us ever closer to reflect the perfect image of Jesus. Continuing to change and living in obedience to His leading in the manner of Jesus, is our life's goal and is the ongoing final step. When we accept this process we are at peace with God.

When the peace with God and the peace of God become real to us we can then strive for peace on earth. There is a real paradox present here. While fighting and resisting evil in the world, which includes the people we associate with, we must strive to be at peace with all. To "hate the sin but love the sinner" is our creed. By practicing the love of God in our lives, living at peace becomes real and possible. If someone despises you and seeks you harm it is difficult to be at peace with him. This does not mean that we need to leave ourselves totally defenseless and allow harm to come upon us, but our first intent should be to be at peace with him and try to resolve conflict if possible. This is what Jesus meant when He said to "turn the other cheek."[68]

May the start of the great benediction "May the peace that passes all understanding..." bring into our lives the tranquility and sense of security and well-being that God desires as we live through Him and for Him.

PATIENCE

In today's world of instant everything, instant gratification, instant communication, even instant pudding, it is easy to see that patience is in short supply. The over bearing pace of today's lifestyle coupled with the desire to keep up with the Jones, in the midst of a society that has lost its sense of decency, is daunting to say the least. The pleasure seeking crowd has lost its conscience bringing immorality and crudeness to the stage of everyday life. This results in short tempers and rage which leads to bitterness. It is little wonder then that we experience "road rage" and "drive-by shootings." Few ever show tolerance for one another and fewer still show love.

---

68   Mathew 5:39

Patience as listed in the fruit of the Spirit, is not just waiting for good to come about, it is translated from Greek to mean "slow wrath, or long suffering." Long suffering means that we look past our short sightedness of present situations, to the glory to be experienced in heaven. To show steadfast endurance through every time of trial and suffering we encounter during our lifetime. To exhibit a tolerant and a caring attitude toward those who treat us badly. Setting aside our emotions and loving with the love of God is needed to practice patience. This entails making the decision to love and respond to all with an attitude that promotes civility, reconciliation, while pointing to our source, God the Father. All encounters should be met with the concept that this person is so loved by God that He sent Jesus to die for him. All are potential brothers or sisters in Christ, and not opponents to be belittled or defeated.

Slow to anger does not mean no anger at all; it means dealing with anger in the proper way. God gave us the emotion of anger to respond to the circumstances He hates; this being willful rejection of Him, His ordinances, and those to whom He has called to be His own. Handling anger is shown though several methods. Some react with immediate and violent rage, always assuming malevolence from the provoker. This leads to an equal response from the opposing person which further escalates tension. Continued separation is the consequence making reconciliation nearly impossible. Repressing or suppressing anger by holding it inside is also wrong. No visible outrage is displayed, but the culmination of this pent up anger often leads to serious disease or depression, or a violent eruption severing relationships. Both of these approaches are ungodly and unhealthy.

The patience of the Spirit is handling anger correctly. Impeding negative reactions to someone or circumstance gives time to seek the reason for conflict, and by never assuming malevolence by the offending party, we seek civil resolutions to whatever confronts us. Such pause gives time to see the situation through the eyes of others and time to discern a problem that may have led them to this negative response. It also gives us a chance to regroup and plan how we may minister to them. It takes the focus off of us and places it on those who may need ministering. Even if they refuse an offer of friendship or help, it brings joy and honor to God as His children exhibit fruitful traits and condemnation on those who refuse. Jesus spoke to Peter of this kind of loving patience when He said to forgive someone seventy times seven times.[69] Patience with tolerance is the glue

---

69   Matthew 18:22

which holds relationships together. It doesn't matter if is in our marriage, our family, our church, or our country, when we do not exhibit patience we struggle with relationships.

KINDNESS

In today's self-absorbed society, few people take the initiative to show kindness to others. With staggering pressure to perform at our job and in our relationships, stress levels mount to a tremendous level causing lack of kindness to even close family members or even pets. A common reason for lack of kindness to anyone is the amount of time and effort required. It is seen as a sacrifice to be friendly toward others, especially when we would prefer to just ignore them and pass by quickly. Action is required if we look to be kind to others. Kindness is proactive, not reactive. The act of kindness can only happen when a positive action is made toward others. Passivity is not kindness, but lack of conflict is what some settle for.

Often our current narcissistic culture only looks at what is potentially beneficial to ourselves. It places little value on anyone or anything that does not show immediate results from our efforts. In addition the risk of rejection becomes involved by showing kindness, as others misinterpret our motives. All have experienced the pain from some form of rejection in their lives, so avoiding it is natural. Further risk involves becoming a target of abuse and manipulation by those who may have evil in their hearts. This should never be used as an excuse to not be kind. We should be optimistic and assume that what is offered will be accepted in the spirit with which it was given. When we act benevolently toward others we are making a decision. It is the decision to be involved with others and enhance their lives. It means taking an active role in lives and proclaiming the love of the One who indwells us to the glory of God the Father.

Even repeated rejection must not thwart willingness to risk showing kindness toward those with a hard heart. Kindness may be the only way to penetrate the thick layers of defense erected by someone in pain. Kindness may melt that hard heart and bring forth a loving friend who may then seek and serve the Lord. Showing the wrath of God towards sin and holding someone on the brink of hell is useful in some situations, but the Love and grace of God through kindness is a far more effective way to reach the stubborn, wounded, and hard of heart.

Kindness can be shown through sympathy or empathy. Sharing like experience can bring to remembrance what was helpful in resolving our own difficulties. Even trivial problems call for our empathy and love to share the burden. If we have not shared a similar experience before, our imagination becomes useful to comprehend and plan a solution. God gave us a brain and emotions to help in resolving problems, especially those of a fellow believer. Circumstances may demand just our presence to allow venting or grieving. The fact that care is expressed is often enough to help someone through hardships or grief.

Kindness is the action of the love of God. If we truly want the best for others, we need to be active and try to instill God's best to all.

GOODNESS

Most people believe that they are good. Goodness in today's vernacular is subjective to each person's interpretation. Most think that the opposite of good is evil, so if they are not evil they must be good. This has been the debate throughout history, with many descriptions being offered. Some have said that good is the experience of pleasure and the removal of pain and suffering. This is flawed thinking because the thing that causes the removal of pain and suffering is not always good. Think of the abuse of drugs, alcohol, or indulgent sex. Others hold wisdom and education as the pinnacle of goodness. Again this is flawed as some of the inmates in prison are highly educated, and Satan is extremely knowledgeable. Even the golden rule is suspect when it allows each individual to be the arbiter of what is good. Some say that good is the greatest benefit for the most people. This sounds fine unless you are one in the minority. Finally, many people today believe that good is having enough possessions to make them happy, so they may live the "good life." Again this leaves each to determine what or how much is enough and good.

Mankind, on his own, is incapable of defining good. We are short sighted and evil by nature, making judgments to our benefit and not as God would. We feed our pride and arrogance with the justification that we instinctively know good. God and God alone is good. This was told to us by Jesus as He spoke to the rich young Jew who called Jesus good.[70] All our standards, morals, and ethics must come from God, who is neither corrupt nor bound by evil and selfish ways. To have goodness is to live in God's will and seek revelation of His divine goodness. We anticipate the day when all God has created will again be called good, and each of His people hears "well done thou *good* and faithful servant."

---

70   Mark 10:18

FAITHFULNESS

Faithfulness is a word seldom used today. It is generally mentioned in the passing of a loyal dog, because of his unconditional love, or at other times it deals with long term relationships; an anniversary or perhaps a retirement party. Unfortunately, today's society seldom puts the required time and effort to become faithful. Faithfulness develops from something being totally trusted over a long period of time. We trust that we will have air to breathe each morning as we arise because it has proved true all our lives. We trust the other drivers on the road to follow traffic regulations because we have seldom if ever been in a collision. We trust that our spouse will remain by our side through all the trials of life. When something is consistent for a period of time, we begin to trust in it. We begin to have the assurance that the consistency shown will continue and therefore it becomes faithful to us and we begin to return faithfulness.

Humans survive on trust. It was instilled into us by our Creator so we could trust Him. The earth God created is faithful to us. It is suspended in space with no means of support, and turns on its axis and travels around the sun to provide us days and seasons. Its ecosystems provide food and resources for our needs and pleasure. The laws of physics and gravity are constant to the point we can rely on them. It is no wonder then that as humans we are built to have faith in things that have shown to be faithful. Therefore, we seek things and people who have shown the consistency to allow trust to develop.

As imperfect beings, we struggle to be consistent in our lives. Qualities deserving of great admiration are present at one point and the most vile the next. This is overcome by anchoring ourselves into something that is unchanging and always perfect. The only thing that qualifies for such a position is the Triune God of creation. Only when we can fix our eyes on someone who is unchangeable and forgiving of our faults, can we hope to become as solid in our lives.

By living in the will of God with consistency by trust and assurance we become full of faith, reaching a solid level of faithfulness to God and to others who look to us as an example. When we reside in the will of God we can have faith in Him throughout all life's trials and tribulations. The faith of Christ Himself is imparted to us through the presence of the Holy Spirit. We then become defenders of the faith and truth even unto martyrdom with joy and peace. We can endure and run the race of life to its glorious climax when we return home to our God.

MEEKNESS

In today's culture meekness is often seen as weakness. No one wants to be seen as weak or timid, because to the world this means failure. Everyone strives to be strong and fearless. Meekness as listed in the fruit of the Spirit is certainly not weak or timid. Words that are more analogous with meekness are humility and gentleness. To be meek is to have a quiet confidence in the strength and abilities we possess, because of whom we belong to, and who dwells within us. To be meek is never having to prove our worth, value, or strength to man because we have already been accepted by God. Gentleness can be seen in a grandpa on the floor wrestling with his grandson. Even though the older man is much more powerful, he is very gentle in the handling of the younger to the point of allowing him to win. Grandpa sees no need of demonstrating superior strength and enjoys the success of his progeny.

Often is heard the loud bragging of past exploits to bolster egos. All too often others wave their credentials as a symbol of worth and value. All of this speaks of weakness and lack of self assurance. The true representation of accomplishment is not what we have acquired or achieved but by how we live. With the calm self assurance revealed in the scripture, "When God is for us who can be against us,"[71] we live our lives with tenderness and compassion for others. A life lived in this fashion brings a difference in us that others notice and comment on. Living in God's strength tempered by meekness allows us to set an example to be emulated by others while not promoting ourselves. The goal of living is not to seek glory for ourselves, but to bring glory to Him that owns us. We further God's kingdom by the quiet strength used to lovingly proclaim the Gospel to the unsaved around us.

SELF-CONTROL

Self-control means to hold in check all that would detract from serving God in the freedom He has given us. It is the part of the fruit which we have the most control over, for it is the on-going decisions we make daily. It also entails our choice to repent of our continuing sin and returning to serving God. The definition of the Greek word used here is self-mastery. Have you ever seen a wild animal that has been caged, set free? The animal takes off in blind flight never considering the consequences to itself. We are also free from the guilt and consequences of our sin, but we should not

---

71   Romans 8:31

take off in any direction without the Spirit's guidance. We should be aware that with freedom comes responsibility, because it can also be abused and lead to a life of excess.

Life in the freedom of Christ has been a struggle since the days of the early church, Some try to limit the possible abuse of freedom by establishing strict ethical codes, a list of the dos and don'ts to be followed. Others have fallen into living for pleasure to the point of excess. One is called legalism and the other is called hedonism. The path of Godly living is in between these two perils. By swerving a little to either side we are at risk of becoming unrighteous and unable to be used in God's eternal plan. The guidance of the Holy Spirit will keep us exactly in the center of God's will.

God has set the standards of behavior that are right and lead to righteousness. We are to say yes to what He has ordained, and no to what He has forbidden, for on our own we are incapable of discerning and implementing these things. That is why God has given us the Holy Spirit to lead us into knowledge, and empower us to be over-comers. All the acts of sinful nature previously listed will be removed by the working of the Holy Spirit. All the segments of the fruit of the Spirit will show forth as the Holy Spirit recreates us. Self-control can be best summed up by the words of Christ in the garden of Gethsemane, "Not my will but Thine be done."[72]

THE GREAT EXAMPLE

Each aspect of the fruit of the Spirit is unique but inseparable from the others. Each builds on and enhances the other, creating a whole and healthy person. They work together to produce the kind of people we should be in the body of Christ. Some may be fearful of being incapable of producing and displaying fruit, but it is not up to us. It is the joy and pleasure of the Holy Spirit to produce fruit in the lives of the believer. It is our job to keep choosing to submit and be obedient to the leading of the Spirit and the will of the Father.

Can we recall knowing or hearing of anyone who exhibited all the segments of the fruit of the Spirit? Of course we can. That person was Jesus Christ! He revealed the glory and nature of God the Father. If Jesus exhibited both the fruit and God, are not they of the same essence? The fruit of the Spirit is the nature and character of God. God is love and it is

72   Matthew 26:39

displayed in His creation. God is joyful and takes delight in all who return to Him. God is peace as He displays in the tranquil order He set forth in creation. God is patient, holding off His terrible judgment until all have had a chance to repent and return to Him. God is kind in the actions He has taken to show His love and mercy. God is the very definition of goodness. God is faithful and always constant in His works. God is meek and gentle by the way He holds back His wrath, for all deserve the fires of hell. God is surely self control and controls every aspect of the universe through His will

As we strive to live a life of submission to God, we begin to take on His nature by displaying the fruit of the Spirit. This allows God to use us in sometimes supernatural ways to bring unbelievers to Him and build up and edify all in His body. Others see the beauty of the fruit and begin to seek the means by which they may also bear fruit, leading them to God through Jesus. This proliferation of believers blesses us and brings glory to God.

POINTS TO PONDER

1. What must happen in my life to be fruitful?

2. What kind of fruit can I produce for Jesus?

3. What are the implications of John 15, for being fruitful?

8

PREPARE TO BE GIFTED!

Everyone at some time or another has held a "hero" in high esteem. In the days before today's mass media it was probably a figure in ancient lore or someone in our community or family. Perhaps the heroic feats preformed by God through His servants as shown in the Bible, were the source of our heroes. Whoever they were, they were attributed with larger than life abilities and wisdom, with strength and courage to match. We aspired to live as they did and may have even pretended to be them. Failure to emulate them fully was common, so fantasizing about having super human gifts, talents, and abilities became a favorite pastime.

In today's world there are not only heroes but super heroes. They are found in every direction we turn, from cartoons to sports. As children we (who are a little older) wanted to be like Popeye. We truly thought that eating spinach would give us bulging muscles to fight our Blutos. Or perhaps it was Superman we envied. Fantasizing being able to fly, or use other super-human abilities to save the heroine from the villain, was our secret ambition. Today kids may be watching the Ninja Turtles and the Power Rangers. In every generation we long to have the ability that sets us above others, and gives us a sense of accomplishment and worth.

Maybe as we aged our heroes became sports figures. We dreamed of having the ability to outrun our rivals, or sink the last second shot to win the game. The fame and fortune while being revered as idols was very alluring to us mere mortals. Perhaps we tried to sink the winning shot but failed miserably, and instead of becoming the hero we became the brunt of scorn and ridicule. Realization began to set in as we learned that our heroes were gifted beyond the norm, and we were incapable of aping their performances.

Even as adults we admire and envy our heroes whether they are successful business entrepreneurs, or astronauts. Those who are gifted with the ability to predict market trends, who are great orators, or who are highly intelligent capture our fancy. We envy their success, and strive to duplicate their accomplishments.

This coveting is not limited to talents or abilities. There may be a desire for appearance or personality. Many desire a different face, hair, weight, or any of a myriad of more "desirable" body features. That is why there are so many diets and self improvement fads, not to mention a waiting list to see a plastic surgeon. Popularity is heaped upon those who are beautiful, those who have the right friends, or those who come from the correct neighborhood. Why do we crave what others have been blessed with? Why are we seldom content with what God has graced us? He has molded us into creatures perfect to fulfill His specific plan for each, so why aren't we satisfied with all God has given?

The reason is clear. Mankind has a sinful nature inherited from the fall that seeks to promote and worship self. We are all guilty of coveting. The gifts and abilities longed for are not to glorify God and help others as He intended, as much as they are to elevate ourselves. Very few of the "heroes" we idolize actually use their fame and wealth to help others less fortunate as God intended. Even fewer give thanks, let alone praise, to God for their status and blessings. Often the true motive for their generosity, if they exhibit any, is the positive publicity they receive, which again elevates and strokes their egos. If we would only understand that the reason God grants all of us talents, (some being special), is to bring glory to Him and further His Kingdom, we would find the satisfaction and worth we crave.

WE ARE GIFTED

Many have sought success, fame, and fortune their entire lives, only to suffer repeated failure. Without success and often without moral support, some may stop striving. Recurring disappointments may generate feelings of inadequacy and rejection. They may even lead some to believe that they are not gifted or talented enough to make a difference in their own lives, so surly not in the lives of others. Often the fear of rejection harshly experienced causes some to resign themselves to accept mediocrity, settling for much less than God intended. All we see is what we don't have, and covet what we perceive others possess.

The good news is that God has made each of us precisely to be able to do everything He intends us to do. From before creation, God had a plan for each of us and gives us what we needed to complete His plan. He gives each the talents and gifts needed to become the perfect instrument for Him to use to achieve what He wills through us. He orchestrates our entire lives, and can even use our mistakes to put us into a position from which we can complete His mission. Our part is to surrender totally to Him and accept His authority and divine guidance.

God has made each of us distinctly unique. No two people share the same finger prints. That is just an obvious difference. No two people, other than identical twins, have the same DNA. Every aspect of our being is unique. Our physical appearances are obviously different, but we also have differences in our minds and souls. Some are gifted in the arts, others in science. Our character also differs greatly. Some are introverted, others are extroverted. Some are naturally quiet and shy, others are bold and brash. The blending of these traits could fill volumes, but the idea is to be aware of the fact that we were created just as God planned, and we should glory in that fact. God intended some to be bold leaders, accomplishing mighty deeds in submission to His guidance. But not every one is called to monumental undertakings. God, in His sovereignty, chooses everyone to fulfill His purpose whether it is slaying Goliath or rocking a baby. That we are obedient with love is far more important than what deeds we do. That we trust God enough to answer His call with humility brings to Him much more glory and honor than just doing the deed.

A PART OF THE WHOLE

Imagine for a moment that we were all created alike, except for gender. If we all had precisely the same strengths and weaknesses how could we ever be able to solve a problem? If one person could not arrive at an answer no one else could either. How could we give advice or comfort to those we love if they thought the same exact way? How could a puzzle be assembled if all the pieces were identical? Unless we were all created perfectly we could not survive. In fact, we were created as perfect beings. We were perfect in design for our tasks when in union with God, with our mates close by our side. But He also wanted to let that be our choice, so He gave us free will to choose. Our pride and vanity led us to the fall from grace, and our need for one another became necessary to just survive. We are social creatures by nature and we need the strengths of others to reach our full potential.

The Scripture uses a beautiful metaphor to describe this. The church of Jesus Christ is called His "body."[73] We can all understand the way a *healthy* body functions. Each part does its function in perfect harmony with the rest. No part ever complains about not being a more important part, and never desires to be moved to a different duty. Say for instance, the skin on our wrist begins to itch. Every part of the body responds to resolve the problem because the entire body is irritated. The nerves send a signal to the brain to inform it of the problem. The brain tells the eyes to look at the area for possible causes. But to do this, the head must swivel and the arm must turn to allow observation. If nothing is found the brain then tells the opposite arm to reach over near the suspect area. The fingers are then instructed to move back and forth to scratch the area. In the end the whole body is relieved and gratified for having done its part. This is an over simplification of the extraordinary complexity of the amazing human body, but it serves to point out how the church is suppose to function, with Jesus as the brain, and all the rest of us working out His edicts. When irritation occurs, the entire body takes steps to alleviate the nuisance. In like manner when one part of the body celebrates, the entire body revels with joy and gladness.

God has given gifts and talents to be used in our lives and in His service. Even an autistic child has been gifted with a gentle spirit that exhibits warmth and affection and an ability to love that few others possess. Our biggest problem is the same one which caused the fall. We are not content with what we have been given, we want more. We want something we *perceive* to be better. Menial tasks are beneath our dignity when we covet being the "superstar." We are trapped into believing we have been cheated and pursue unhealthy and immoral means to possess what we want, never being satisfied with having our needs met. God has blessed all with gifts. Some are gifted physically, some mentally, and some spiritually, while others have multiple gifts. Whatever the gift, it is perfect for everything God has purposed for us to do. Success in God's plan requires identifying the gifts, understanding their uses, and applying them boldly as the Holy Spirit directs. Contentment, with thanksgiving, is experienced as our gifts are used to help others and glorify God. That is stewardship.

73   1 Corinthians 12:12-26

SPECIAL GIFTS OF VOCATION

God gives natural physical and mental abilities diversely to everyone in varying degrees. He does however give special gifts to those who are members of the living body of Jesus Christ, through the indwelling Holy Spirit. He gives them for the development, education, and edification of the body of believers, the church, in preparing them in unity for service.

Some believers are called aside to be pastors as their vocation to the full time service of the body of Jesus Christ. This is a special calling and is prayerfully questioned with diligence, not only by that particular person but by other mature Christians. A man with this calling is also confirmed by the hierarchy of the church before being accepted to serve a body of believers, and is expected to conform to the standards mentioned in Paul's epistle to Timothy.[74] God gives many diverse, special gifts to these who lead their congregation to the knowledge of the truths of God and of His standard of perfection Jesus Christ.

God, through the Holy Spirit, commissions others with gifts of extended duration. Apostles, prophets, evangelists, and teachers are gifted not only for a special event or season, but are identified by the gifts they exemplify. These too may be set apart in the body for full time ministry. The Holy Spirit working in and through them is to reveal the truth concerning God and His eternal plan, to glorify Jesus, and to prepare and empower all in the body to fulfill the great commission, bringing His kingdom ever closer.

The mission and duty of the church is not just the responsibility of the clergy however. Every member has been given a role to play and responsibility to uphold both in the body of believers, and in their own lives. Therefore God, through His Holy Spirit, gives gifts as He sees fit and at His discretion to reveal truths, to teach, to heal, and to uplift and unite us. These are called the Gifts of the Holy Spirit.

GIFTS OF THE HOLY SPIRIT

The Holy Scriptures opens to us the gifts that the Holy Spirit bestows on whom He pleases. There are many gifts but all have the same giver.[75] Every gift is given to enlighten, empower, and unify the body of Christ to execute the great commission and become the spotless bride for the return of the King of Kings. Gifts of the Holy Spirit may be asked for, but only

---

74   1 Timothy 3:1-7
75   1 Corinthians 12:4

a humble, obedient servant will be the vessel filled with power and grace. The book of 1 Corinthians chapter 12 lists these gifts:

The word of wisdom: A word of wisdom is inspired knowledge which focuses on deeper understanding. This may pertain to the truth of Holy Scriptures pointing to the intended essence. It may be a revelation of a fact about a specific situation, insight into prayer needed, or means to make an educated decision. It may be a revelation of the relationship of the Trinity or the unity there contained. No one can limit what God may reveal to anyone, but precaution must be taken. The lies and deceit of Satan must always be guarded against and rebuked, as he masquerades as an angel of light.[76] Look to God's nature and character for direction in discerning what is from Him. God's word never changes, and therefore what ever is revealed in words of wisdom will always be inline with and confirmed by the Holy Scriptures.

The word of knowledge: A word of knowledge is the progressive movement toward understanding all God is. It discloses His divine attributes and character with more clarity than we can learn without His assistance. It also moves us ever more closely into the likeness of Jesus Christ, so our impact on the environment we occupy may be touched with the grace of the Eternal Savior. Words of knowledge deepen and strengthen our love and desire to grow into His likeness.

Faith: This faith does not ask for a choice (to believe or not believe), it is the strength of conviction which allows saints to go beyond logic. Simple faith is the result of gathering information, pro and con, to determine whether or not to believe. This is the faith that brings people to choose to submit to Jesus Christ and allow Him to become their Lord and Savior. The gift of faith is absolute confidence in our position with God and goes beyond reason or normality. The gift of faith allows a saint bravely to pray for his executioner as he prepares to strike. The gift of faith gives a saint the courage to stand in battle against overwhelming odds, or lay down his life for others. God will help His faithful to be over-comers with the gift of faith.

The gift of healing: When God decides to set something back into proper order, He can and will empower His faithful servant to perform in His authority. Healing can occur where ever God's natural order is askew. This may be, as most of us think, in the physical body. However, healing is often needed in other areas as well since the human being is a very complex creature. Healing is sometimes needed not only in our physical bodies, but

---

76   2 Corinthians 11:14

in out souls and spirits. At times healing is needed between people and in strained or broken relationships.

Being such short-sighted creatures, we often presume to "know" what is right and how events "should" turn out. This is foolishness because we do not see the entire picture and how God is furthering His plan. He will heal in one of four ways. He may miraculously heal through His power. He may choose to heal through counseling or therapy. He may wish to use others such as doctors to bring about our healing. Or, He may decide to set someone completely free from disease by calling them to His heavenly realm. However God wishes to intervene in our health is absolutely perfect and in accordance with His actions, will, and timing.

The working of miracles: God has established His order in this world in which we live. His ways are so natural to the routine of all creation that we expect them to repeat themselves over and over again. However, being the Creator gives Him the right to disrupt and supercede natural order as He desires. He shows His power and glory in the miracles He displays, and establishes who His saints are in this process. Miracles are not limited to great earth shaking events. They may be as small as a "coincidence" meeting with someone you have needed to see. It may be as important as your loved one coming to Christ after countless times of rejecting Him. Always expect God to be working, sometimes in ways that are both unexpected and powerful.

Prophecy: When prophecy is mentioned, it is often presumed that some prediction is given. This is only one part of what prophecy is. When the Spirit leads someone to prophesy they speak out of the mind and council of God. This may be His telling of His will or purpose in the past, present, or future. What ever He wishes to convey to His people may be relayed through a prophet. God speaks directly to His people to comfort and exhort them, bring reassurance of His faithfulness and love. He can also use prophecy to convict and convert non-believers to become members of Christ's body and His own sons and daughters. Whoever prophesizes is in fact speaking for God.

Discerning of spirits: Every living being, whether angelic or human, has been created with a spirit. It is the means by which creation can associate with the Divine. These creatures were given free choice by God, who wanted an offering of love and obedience voluntarily, not by coercion or fabrication. Having free will shows that they have a mind to decide, a will to carry out their choice, and emotions to validate or convict them for their actions. These are elements of a soul. Unlike angels, humans have a physical body fixed in time and space. Choices made with free will affect the entire being with all of its parts. Choice leads to the condition of being with God (good) or being without Him (evil).

In the events of our lives we are constantly besieged with good and evil. Often evil can be deceiving to the point of appearing good, when in reality it can cause great harm and even death. The Holy Spirit can gift extraordinary ability to distinguish the intent and source of spirits, weather in a human, an angel, or in a demon. This gift also allows a saint to discover and partake in the spirit of Christ. Discerning intentions and motives of those who call themselves Christians is included here, alerting the saint of possible risk and danger. Empowered by the knowledge discernment brings, we can act and plan for action accordingly when facing difficult events.

Speaking in tongues: At Pentecost, the Holy Spirit came upon the saints gathered, with great power, using their voices to utter truth to others in their native language. This is known as the gift of tongues. Through the years the need for tongues has diminished because of education and better communication. Now that the gospel has been written, reading replaces some direct preaching. Also, evangelists are better prepared to go to a region to preach in that they either pre-learn the language or hire an interpreter. This doesn't mean that God can't use tongues any more; He may choose to use it, but sparingly. He is sovereign and does what is in His will to do. It is His will to use the myriad of ways to further His eternal plan. Today when the gift of tongues is given during group meetings, it is accompanied by the gift of interpretations. This is the ability for hearing and translating all which is spoken in foreign languages into an understandable language revealing the truth the Spirit is imparting.

Another form of speaking in tongues occurs, but is mentioned less frequently. This is the tongues of a private prayer language that the Spirit uses to convey deep utterances and petitions to God the Father. The Spirit uses this prayer to remove the bias and confusion of a saint from the commune with Him. It edifies the person praying, so it is very personal. The Spirit knows our needs better than we do and expresses them in such a way that a human mind can't interfere.

The gifts of the Spirit are primarily to build up, train, comfort, and edify the body of Christ. Seldom are these gifts used other than for the body, so speaking in tongues in an assembly of the body is not profitable without an interpretation. Likewise the prayer language of tongues is not for the group, but more for the individual. In 1 Corinthians chapter 14 the

Apostle Paul shows the priorities and the importance of the gifts to bring the body of Christ into a spotless bride for our returning King.

Interpretation of tongues: Speaking in tongues is not as significant to the welfare of the body of Christ as other gifts are. However, God can use the gift of tongues along with its interpretation to not only benefit the whole but also to build the importance of working with and trusting fellow members of the body. By partnering saints together, the Spirit nurtures shared commitment and resolve to carry on. Interpretation is not limited to the translation of the gift of tongues, it, in general, is to convey the meaning or truth of any communication from God, verbal, written, or by visions and dreams.

Intended for the education, maturation, healing, and empowering of saints, the gifts of the Holy Spirit are often manifested in groups. The number is not as relevant as the hearts of those attending. God asks for pure, loving saints submitted to furthering His kingdom and giving Him the glory that is His. The extent to which God through His Holy Spirit manifests His gifts and powers to His children is limitless, as other books in the New Testament indicate. Not exhibiting the manifestations of the gifts listed above is not an indication of the lack of receiving spiritual gifts. Galatians chapter 5 lists hospitality as a gift of the Spirit, and certainly interceding in prayer for others is a gift. The gifts are all equal in importance and the joy of using them in obedience is truly rewarding. Truckloads of books could not contain the ways God uses His people to further His plan, but these basic precepts are true and offered to give some insight into the ways we are to be empowered to do His bidding.

We don't need to be superstars to be gifted; in fact, humility combined with a servant's heart is how we are able to be "great" in the kingdom of God and allow the Holy Spirit to manifest His power through these gifts.

POINTS TO PONDER

1. How willing am I to be 'gifted' by God?

2. Am I ready to be God's gift to others?

3. What gift would I like God to give me?

9

PREPARE TO BE SALT AND LIGHT!

Of all creation, mankind is the only creature who is particular in the taste of its sustenance. Other species may have preferences in food, but nothing is passed over if it readily available. Unless we are near starvation, we choose to consume only what our palate considers tasty. Even in this most basic need and function of our lives, we reveal our greed and self advancement by demanding what we want, regardless of whether it is healthful or not. Mankind alone uses spices to enhance the taste of food to his liking. Different cultures use different spices in unique combinations, but salt is used universally. Perhaps adding flavor is the attribute of salt that Jesus Christ attributed to His followers when He called them the "salt of the earth".[77] Perhaps we, by being salt, give flavor and tolerability to this evil and corrupt world allowing our Heavenly Father to patiently await the time to fulfill His plan. Conversely perhaps by being salt, we in the body of Christ can give to those in the world a taste of freedom from the pain and bondage this world gives; a taste of the glorious fellowship with God through the acceptance of Jesus Christ as Lord and Savior. This is a mere sampling of the Great Feast that awaits His own in heaven and may be savored now.

---

77   Matthew 5:13

Christ called us the salt of the earth right after He described the characteristics of being like Him in the beatitudes. When we exhibit these traits we begin the transformation of becoming a new creature with a specific purpose. If we do not exhibit these traits, we have never truly been salt as He defined it. When salt is used, it is for a specific purpose. If salt (or one of us) does not fulfill its purpose it is not really salt, and is worthless, and is "thrown out and trampled by men".

Pure salt has a distinctive taste. Salt which contains other minerals becomes impure and its taste can become altered, but pure salt is unmistakable. Impurities can coat the outside layer of salt which hides its taste, but they cannot remove salt's true essence. Salt can be diluted or its taste hidden, but pure salt tastes salty, or it is something else. Likewise, the true members of Christ's body can not lose their saltiness. They too can be made impure by false doctrine and deceptions, and become hidden by outside influences or apathy. If they do, their testimony is diminished and tainted and is useless for furthering the kingdom of Christ. The evil one is a master of deceiving whoever is not vigilant and strongly rooted in the truth of scripture. He is constantly trying to taint the purity of the saints to diminish their effectiveness for God. Thankfully, both salt and the body of Christ can be refined and purified back to its uncontaminated state.

THE NATURE OF SALT

God has given salt the characteristic of attracting and retaining water. In a living creature salt regulates the water in the body, preserving adequate amounts to allow proper cellular function. Salt is essential for every animal, but toxic to plants. Salt is so essential for healthy animals that ranchers provide salt licks for their livestock, and in the wild, creatures seek out natural salt licks. Conversely, plant life is so negatively affected by salt that it was used in ancient times to lay waste to the food growing fields of enemies. As with many beneficial things in life, a proper balance is needed. Too much, or too little salt can lead to serious problems. It's not coincidental that most bodily fluids contain a saline solution (salt and water). Blood, sweat, and tears all are all salty for this reason.

Water retention is analogous in the Christian body as well. Nothing in creation lives without water. The people of Jesus' day were very much aware of this and a shortage of water was critical. Rainfall was seen as a blessing from God and a sign of His good favor, refreshing both man and countryside. Old Testament prophets described Yahweh as "the fountain of living waters"[78] and it is repeated in the New Testament in relationship to Jesus through the Holy Spirit.[79] Water was also used in many ways for regular and ceremonial cleansings commanded by God for His people Israel. Later, water was used in baptism for the cleansing of sins through repentance and for initiation and incorporation into Jesus Christ.

Water was, and still is at the heart of any healthy community, and its benefits and value are again being revived and retold. All in the body of Christ are the salt which retains the water of baptism, the cleansing and life giving water given by God, satisfying the burning thirst of a world filled with death.

For countless ages salt was used as a preservative. Before the invention of canning or refrigeration, salt was the most common way to preserve meat and fish. Rubbing the meat with salt initially removed excess moisture. It is in this moisture that bacteria thrive and reproduce resulting in rotting and rapid decomposition of the meat. Salt also dehydrates the bacteria cells which results in their death. Our ancestors discovered this and used salt to disinfect wounds. (Ouch!!)

The body of Christ is also very much a preservative in today's world. It is through the presence of the Holy Spirit in His body that He resides from age to age. It is through the body of Christ that the life giving, eternal water is made available to all who choose to accept it. Without the presence of the Holy Spirit in the body of Christ, evil would not be resisted and fought. Without the body of Christ, prayers for the blessings and changes brought about by our loving God would not come about.

Salt has been valued throughout history. Wars have been fought over it. Large towns have developed around its mining and refining centers. Trade routes were established primarily for its trade. In Biblical times salt was rare enough that it was used as currency. In today's modern world, salt is plentiful. Science has discovered vast stores of salt, and has advanced its mining and refining. However, in remote regions of the world salt can still be scarce, and hence valuable.

Salt is a very stable compound, and the church is called to have a stabilizing influence in the world. Since we have the blessing of being in the family of the almighty Creator and Father of all, we should exude an air of confidence and peace in being solidly assured of His promises, thereby establishing a stable foundation of hope.

The body of Christ is truly the salt of the Earth. The world craves and

---

78   Jeremiah 2:13
79   John 4:10

spends its time seeking the truth given by its Creator without knowing what it wants. Deep in the hearts of all humans lies something always sought; a means to live without pain and suffering while being free from fear and death. They seek love and acceptance with the assurance that they have reason and purpose in living. They need God who is love and gives peace, hope, and security. Sadly, the world is too easily deceived and led astray, thus finding the Gospel of Jesus Christ too simplistic or too antiquated to believe. Everyone universally craves to be loved and needed. Everyone universally craves and needs salt to live. Could there be a correlation between the two? God is love, and He and Jesus are one. We, who proclaim Jesus as the Son of God and atonement for all sin, are one in Him through the indwelling of His Holy Spirit. We are the reservoir and dispenser of God's love in this world. We are the functioning heads, hearts, and hands of our Lord to bring His love to all mankind. Let us forever be salty.

LET THERE BE LIGHT

The word light conjures up many different meanings to people at various times, and well it should. Light in the English language is an amazingly diverse word. The *Funk and Wagnall's Standard Desk Dictionary* lists 62 definitions for light. It can be used as a noun, or as a verb to show action. It can be used as an adjective to describe, as well as becoming an adverb by adding ly. The English definition of light ranges from igniting a flame to something less filling: from illumination to humorous. In Greek the word is phos and is defined as light (means of illumination) or fire. When Christ called His saints the "light of the world",[80] He was referring to this definition.

The most popular and frequently used meaning of the word light is illumination. The first definition listed in the previously mentioned dictionary is: "the form of radiant electromagnetic energy that stimulates the organs of sight." It then proceeds to mention the non-visible radiant energy, ultraviolet and infrared light which contain countless particles moving in an assortment of wave lengths. All creatures that possess normally functioning eyes can use visible light reflected from any object to observe and know their surroundings, but are unaware of the accompanying non-visible light. Extraordinary means of detection are needed to perceive the presence of the non-visible waves of energy. The same is true with the spiritual realm.

---

80   Matthew 5:14

Light may be visible or invisible, but still often incomprehensible to all but the ones to whom God reveals it.

ILLUMINATION

Light emanates from some form of energy or power. Without an energy source no light is present and this condition is known as darkness. Darkness is the standard in the universe. Darkness does not overcome light; darkness exists until it is overcome by light. Light penetrates the darkness at a speed faster than any other known object, illuminating everything it falls upon.

As light strikes an object, some light rays are absorbed, and some are reflected. Reflected rays are collected by the eye which sees different wavelengths as different colors. The color of an object is a composite of all the different rays of light which are reflected from the object. Light is composed of three primary, and three secondary colors with the combination thereof giving us all the innumerable shades of color. If an object absorbs all light and none is reflected it is called black. Also if an object reflects all the rays of light, it is called white. Thus, a source of light must emit pure white light if objects are to appear as they truly are.

Light can be as soft as the first hint of daybreak, or the soft glow of a candle. It can also be bright enough to cause blindness with great discomfort. When concentrated, (as with modern lasers) light can cut through steel. Our moods are described with colors, which are segments of white light. When we think of green, we often relate to the early part of spring when plants are fresh and growing. Yellow reminds us of sunshine; red of anger. Blue denotes sadness for many, while purple is the color of royalty. White is the color for clean and sterile, and black is symbolic of evil. Because white is the result of reflecting all rays of light it becomes symbolic of the purity and holiness of the risen saints. Their generosity and love are freely given to all around them with nothing being reserved or hoarded for themselves. Evil is portrayed as black in that it does not reflect but selfishly keeps all for itself. It is obvious that light in all its shades is a bigger part of life than we imagine, and something we take for granted.

God has given plants the ability to use light to transform matter and water into food. Light is the basic element needed to produce food, whether used for the plant itself or if the plant is eaten for food. All life on earth is dependant on the sun not only for food and light, but also warmth, which is emitted from a power source as infrared radiation, a light not in the visual range. Heat is a common by-product of most sources of light that we are familiar with, and the warmth shared by the body of Christ is the result of the source of light within each member.

At creation, after the heaven and earth were formed, the natural state of darkness prevailed. God said "let there be light"[81] and there was light. Light was the first thing God created and saw that "it was good".[82] What is good? Good can only be what God has called good. He is the arbiter of all creation, and what He has called good is truly good. After light came into being, form and function developed by God appeared in all other creation. All of the other parts of creation were called good and were illuminated by light.

Because God gave free choice to some of His creation, wrong choices were made, and evil came forth. Evil cannot subsist in the presence of the Holiness of God, because, just as darkness is the absence of light, so evil is the absence of God. Because Adam and Eve were ashamed of their actions and tried to hide, they were in darkness. The same is true for Satan and his evil horde along with the lost of the earth. The light of God's truth overpowers all darkness leaving nowhere for evil to hide. The truth and holiness of God is what evil shuns, so it slinks to the dreary shadows and dark paths, away from His presence. Evil seeks to destroy or discredit all God's creation, and despises having its actions exposed.

The Greek word phos is also described as fire. Fire can be the power source of illuminating light, but it can also demonstrate passion. Those who are the light of the world have a passion to share the blessings they have been given to all who are lost, as well as fervor to love God by being obedient to His leading. We possess an unquenchable thirst to follow our source and bring all to receive His mercy.

The other qualities of fire can also be attributed to God's elect. Fire has long been a source of warmth and comfort, creating an air of security and wellbeing. Even today one of camping's favorite activities is gathering around the fire to enjoy fellowship with one another. Christ is our warmth and security. Without Him we are doomed to face life and death without help or hope.

---

81   Genesis 1:3
82   Genesis 1:4

LIGHT AS WISDOM

Since creation, light has been the term used to describe wisdom, understanding, and truth. In this illustration, light is seen as ultimate discernment, the means by which truth is either proven or shown to be false. This is known by the fact that God is light. He is the very epitome of wisdom and His is the only truth. He is the power source behind all wisdom and truth and provides illumination to His creation. God's shining glory and purity are described in the Old Testament repeatedly as light.[83] In the gospels, Jesus also witnessed to this truth when He said "I am the light of the world".[84] Even today a novel idea is symbolized by a light bulb.

The beauty of creation is revealed through light, with all its stunning colors and graceful shapes, while revealing God's wisdom of design. His artistic genius is shown in the way He created objects with different textures and qualities which allow them to dazzle us with breath taking colors. God allows us to gain knowledge of the world He has given in this manner. Light enables mankind to read and learn from the Holy Scriptures, our primary means of learning of and functioning in God's will.

Many miracles of Christ involved the restoration of sight. Whether it was performed by the application of mud, or simply a commanding word, those receiving healing were extremely grateful and filled with joyful worship. Every healing given to these people was analogous of the blindness of the nation of Israel concerning their faith and belief in their God. They had so contorted and mangled the beauty of their covenant with God that they did not recognize Him when He came in the flesh. Although they could see His body, they were spiritually blind to all His truths and insights into His laws and ordinances.

Light is also symbolized in scripture as the essence of being. God is the ultimate in quality, quantity, and sequence. He is the source of all creation as he planned in His definitive purpose and willed it into being through His unmatched power, so everything that is good finds its source and existence in Him. He created us as human beings, in His likeness, for relationship with Him. He is the true source of our light. Our becoming His children and walking in the light is further indication of our return to our Source and Creator.

---

83 Isaiah 60:19
84 John 9:5

LIGHT UNTO THE WORLD

When Jesus said, "You are the light of the world", to whom and about whom was He speaking? He was obviously talking to the apostles and others gathered around Him on that mountain side, as He taught the beatitudes. But, was He referring to those is attendance alone? No. Jesus was talking about everyone, present and future who would hear the Gospel of Peace and believe that He was the only way to the Father. He was foretelling the truth about all who were redeemed from the world to become part of God's family and therefore being filled with the Holy Spirit.

As we grow into the love and close fellowship of God, we are His earthly presence, and continually grow stronger and brighter as we draw closer to Him. We, with His direction, are His hands to serve and love the lost. We are His arms to embrace Christian brothers and sisters, and His shoulder for them to cry on. We are also the voice of God who beckons all to abandon this dying world of evil and surrender themselves to His perfect love. We are His conduit for channeling His grace and understanding to all who are lost and in despair.

When Jesus proclaimed that we are light, He also stated; "a city on a hill cannot be hidden. Neither do people light a lamp and but it under a bowl. Instead they put it on its stand, and it gives light to everyone in the house. In the same way, let your light shine before men, that they may see your good deeds and praise your Father in heaven".[85] Each member of the body of Christ is to be bold and highly visible. Every action taken in the life of a believer is to be "good" because it is being scrutinized by others. When the lost see us loving and giving to one another, they see that there is a real difference in the body of believers. When they pursue the reason, God gets all the glory and hopefully another member of His body is produced. If we talk the talk, we must walk the walk.

God has ordained us to be beacons, brightly shining on a hill, pointing the way home for all who are adrift on the sea of confusion and darkness. We are to be the entrance to the harbor of reconciliation and peace through Christ. We are the only hope many will have of hearing the Good News of Jesus and avoiding the pitfalls of this life and fires of eternal damnation. God is the source of the power and light in us and each is a reflection of that beautiful light. We found the light of salvation through someone, and we are called to shine that others might see it also.

---

85   Matthew 5:14-16 NIV

POINTS TO PONDER

1. Salt is seasoning and preservative – in what ways can I be such in the world?

2. Am I a shining light in this dark world?

3. How can I best be salt and light as Jesus said to be?

10

PREPARE TO LIVE VICTORIOUSLY!

If life seems to always be a struggle, that's because it is. We as Christians face many foes who oppose the life to which God calls us. First we fight against God's perpetual enemy Satan and his evil hoard. Then we struggle with a physical body which has been dying from the day we were born. In addition we struggle with the deviant way our minds have thought, trained by the influence of this fallen world. Being the prideful, self loving creatures we are, we burn with desire for everything we want. The battles rage, but the war has already been won. Even though we are positioned on the front line of these battles, we are not responsible for their outcomes because we are members of the body of Christ and He has secured the victory. We can read in Revelations where and how the spiritual war ends. In 1 Corinthians it is written that we will receive a new glorified body[86], and also in 1 Corinthians it is written that we have the mind of Christ.[87] Jesus Christ has already been given the crown of victory over every foe, and he will reign forever. This doesn't mean however that we can foolishly relax our guard, forgetting that we are still in the battle, for the time appointed for total victory has not yet come. Until it does we are wise to

---

86   1 Corinthians 15:52
87   1 Corinthians 2:16

utilize every weapon at our disposal to persist in engaging our enemies amidst the struggle.

In the spiritual realm we are engaged against Satan and His forces. We must don the battle attire we have been given as written about by the apostle Paul. "Finally, be strong in the Lord and in his mighty power. Put on the full armor of God so that you can take your stand against the devil's schemes. For our struggle is not against flesh and blood, but against the rulers, against the authorities, against the powers of this dark world and against the spiritual forces of evil in the heavenly realms. Therefore put on the full armor of God, so that when the day of evil comes, you may be able to stand your ground, and after you have done everything, to stand. Stand firm then, with the belt of truth buckled around your waist, with the breastplate of righteousness in place, and with your feet fitted with the readiness that comes from the gospel of peace. In addition to all this, take up the shield of faith, with which you can extinguish all the flaming arrows of the evil one. Take the helmet of salvation and the sword of the Spirit, which is the word of God."[88] With the full array of armament given to us, we are covered from the tops of our heads to the bottom of our feet. The only area of the body that lacks armament is the back, for as with the Roman Legions, soldiers are to always face the enemy and never turn and run. With total commitment and courage we are thus engaged in a battle which will end with God's victory to savor.

THE FULL ARMOR OF GOD

Paul was in the custody of Rome and surrounded by Roman soldiers at the time he wrote his letter to the Ephesians. It is widely believed his description of God's armor was based on their uniforms with which he was familiar. The first article of armor that was put on was the sash or belt that was used to hold the other pieces of armor in place, and also to store weapons, equipment, and even rations. It was imperative that the belt was in place to keep the weapons of battle readily available as the battle progressed. We are to put on the belt of truth around our waist as an anchoring component of the entire uniform with proper placement of weapons for immediate access as needed.

This battle is not in the physical world, but in the spiritual realm. Therefore we do not put on an actual belt, but metaphorically we are to encircle ourselves with the truth of God upon which we have a platform

---

88   Ephesians 6:10-17 NIV

from which we can engage in conflict. But, what is truth? Truth is *everything God is, says, and does.*[89] All of His wonderful attributes, characteristics, and nature are true. God always puts it on the line, without hesitation or deception. Every word that proceeds from God's mouth is truth, and is what Jesus said we are to live on. (Jesus said; "man does not live by bread alone, but by every word that comes from the mouth of God". He said this in rebuking Satan after His forty day fast while being tempted.)[90] Every action that God calls for is truth in that His will is perfect and His intentions are pure. When we know the source of truth and understand the lessons we are being taught, we can solidly stand our ground and be fully prepared to carry out our orders.

The breastplate of righteousness covers our most vital organs, especially our hearts. We cannot build a breastplate of righteousness for ourselves, for we can never be righteous from any effort we make. It is Jesus and He alone who imputes His righteousness unto to us through His atoning actions on the cross of Calvary. Satan loses his grip on our hearts when we surrender them to God, but he will fight to regain this territory. When we surrender ourselves to Jesus, place Him on the throne of our hearts, and take on His righteousness, we are blessed with the breastplate which defends us from evil attacks and temptations.

Our feet are to be covered with the preparation of the good news of the gospel. We are commissioned to take the gospel to the entire world, and when we are prepared to do so, we will have the ability to stand firm on uneven ground as we confront our enemies, and travel over rough terrain. The sandals wore by the Roman legions had spikes on their soles somewhat like today's athletic shoes. This innovation is credited with giving the Roman soldier a huge advantage while standing against the surge of the opposing army. Our feet are firmly planted on the good news of the Gospel and make us immovable.

The shield of faith is the protective covering we can use to block the assault of Satan's accusations and lies. The faith which makes up our shield is not in our ability or even in the ability of the shield itself. It is the faith in, and of, our Eternal King, and in His promise to His own. We exercise faith when we have allowed it to grow by confidently living in the power given by God. The Roman shield was often covered with cloth which could be wetted to withstand flaming arrows. Our shield is covered also and is

---

89   John 14:6
90   Matthew 4:4 NIV

wetted by the water of our baptism to extinguish the flaming accusations of Satan.[91]

The helmet of salvation protects one of the greatest battlefields, our minds. Satan tries to weaken this defense with doubt and fear. He tries to get us to forget the truth that we are set free from the stain of sin and fear of death. The temptation to revert back to our previous characteristics is his favorite guile. He tries to lead us back to the evil thoughts and mannerisms we fled from when we were saved. We are to take captive every thought and make them obedient[92] to the mind of Christ that began growing in us upon our rebirth in the spirit.

The sword of the spirit is the word of God[93]. Jesus showed the example of how we are to use the word of God to rebuke Satan, by quoting scripture when being tempted in the wilderness.[94] Never forget that Satan also knows scripture, but like every other thing, he takes what is God's and perverts it. Satan has created nothing on his own, but takes the good things of God and bends and twists them to fit his perverse and evil schemes. The word of God is symbolized in scripture as a two edged sword which cuts to the marrow. In Hebrews we read; "For the word of God is living, and active, and sharper than any double-edged sword, it penetrates even to dividing of soul and spirit, joints and marrow; it judges the thoughts and attitudes of the heart."[95] This is the offensive weapon of power we are to arm ourselves with and engage the enemy at every turn. God's word always accomplishes His purpose[96] whether it is used for creation, or for rebuking Satan as Jesus did.

THE NATURAL BODY

The next battle occurs in our physical bodies. Paul tells us; "Flee from sexual immorality. All other sins a man commits are outside his body, but he who sins sexually sins against his own body. Do you not know that your body is a temple of the Holy Spirit, who is in you, whom you have received from God? You are not your own; you were bought at a price. Therefore honor God with your body".[97] Being the residence of the Holy Spirit, we

91	Psalms 91:5
92	2 Corinthians 10:5
93	Revelation 19:15
94	Matthew 4:1-10
95	Hebrews 4:12 NIV
96	Isaiah 55:11
97	1 Corinthians 6:18-20 NIV

are to abstain from all acts which denigrate our bodies and instead strive to become the likeness of Jesus Christ.

Our bodies are living creations requiring several basic needs to stay healthy; food water, and oxygen, as well as exercise and rest to keep strong. All of these things are good unto themselves, but all can be abused. Gluttony is a sin of self-indulgence and greed, while getting drunk "leads to debauchery."[98] It is lust for pleasure that takes over and starts unhealthy and unholy habits. Eating and drinking can be pleasurable, so we covet more and more food or drink, or spend excess time seeking pleasure, neglecting the need for sufficient sleep or rest. It is the mind that says "I will do what brings me pleasure because exercise is painful. I will indulge in food, drink, and merriment to make myself feel good". Everything should be in balance as we learn to control every thought about our physical enclosures. If we listen to our bodies they will tell us when they are hungry, or need rest, but we should not submit to over-indulgences. We should use discerning and make informed decisions as to what we truly need, rather that what we just want. To fulfill the plan and purpose God has for us, we must fight the good fight in preserving health, and controlling the desire of excess to be ready to proceed in life as ordered.

THE MIND

The mind can be the arena of the heaviest battles. As earlier stated, God gives us the choice to be His and obey Him, or to continue to control our own paths. This is especially true in the battle with our minds. We are to be transformed by the renewing of our minds,[99] as our minds are not instantly change at our rebirth in Christ. It is an ongoing process that requires our constant attention to insure that we persevere in our salvation and make proper choices. Three major areas of our minds must be redeemed and transformed if we are to live in victory. These are our thoughts, our desires, and our inflated ideas of status, namely pride.

There is a battle raging for our thoughts. Paul wrote, "We demolish arguments and every pretension that sets itself up against the knowledge of God, and we take captive every thought to make it obedient to Christ."[100] Every thought that enters our minds is to be filtered through the knowledge of the truth that we have learned from our walk as a member of the body of Christ. Every thought that does not honor God, especially if we are aware,

98   Ephesians 5:18
99   Romans 12:2
100   2 Corinthians 10:5 NIV

that is counter to the nature of Jesus Christ is to be rejected as sinful and then forgotten.

Paul also wrote "Finally, brothers, whatever is true, whatever is noble, whatever is right, whatever is pure, whatever is lovely, whatever is admirable--if anything is excellent or praiseworthy--think about such things."[101] When the Holy Spirit lives within us, we have the ability to discern what is good and proper to set our minds on, and the authority to expel all evil and worthless images and impressions.

Doing this is not accomplished quickly or easily. It is a process of learning and training to detect negative thoughts and shorten the span they dwell in our minds before we finally remove them. It is easy to fall back to the ways we used to think, constantly lusting for money, power, and sensual pleasures, while elevating ourselves and demeaning others, for we are daily bombarded by it in a world full of evil and negativity.

Desires are the catalyst for what we strive to acquire. As children we were given a set of morals (good or bad) to influence how we proceeded in living. At some point our sinful nature led us to covet some of the things we were exposed to. They might have been fame and fortune, or simply to own the American Dream of a house, family, and two cars in the garage. Depending of our personal drive and external motivation, we eagerly proceeded to develop a series of steps to obtain what we coveted. These desires became the focal point in our living and steered us through all the twists and turns toward our goals. They were the inspiration to help us get up in the morning and work at a job we detested. They directed our choices in the courses we took in school. They may have even influenced who we dated and eventually married. The drive to gain our desires led us to do everything within our power to at last be "satisfied". This drive was tempered only by our moral values and consciences, and if they are not in alignment with God's, we surely are sinners.

Desires are not limited to just the major wants of a lifetime, but can be simply a craving for instant gratification. These can become the burning thirst for whatever we covet or simply feel deeply about. King David discovered this when he saw Bathsheba and plotted to have her.[102] As we all remember this led to arranging a murder as he tried to hide his initial sin of coveting. It is not a sin to wish to obtain a dream we have had, but it is to be done in compliance with God's ordinances and will.

Whatever the desires of our hearts have been, they must be abandoned

---

101   Philippians 4:8 NIV
102   2 Samuel 11:1ff

if we are to win the battle over them. The only desire we should now pursue with a passion is to be wholly dedicated to loving and serving our Heavenly Father. If we indeed set this as our goal, He will not only make us His sons and daughters, but we will be in a position to receive all the blessings He has promised. We should allow God to set our desires in accordance to His plan, and strive to reach them with the gifts and talents He has given.

Jesus said, "If you remain in me, and my words remain in you, you will ask whatever you desire, and it will be done for you."[103] When we are mature enough to relinquish our desires and even our very lives to our loving Father, He, in is great love and mercy, may grace us with the gift of our desires. We have done nothing to earn it. It is just another example of His grace.

The final battle which takes place in our minds is one we all have in common, that is an over-inflated esteem of ourselves, or pride.[104] We are taught from an early age to try to excel in what ever we do. We studied to be the smartest in school; we practiced intently to be a good athlete, and we strove to be number one in a host of other examples. When some success was achieved, we may have begun to feel elevated above others. Perhaps we felt it was our right to be treated specially and set above. If this was true we began to covet more power, fame, or money, and we became greedy. Enough was never enough and we schemed up ways to acquire more and more. It is not wrong to attempt to excel, but as with many things we seldom do so in balance. When others are degraded or put down others by our actions it is wrong. When certain chores and assignments are unfulfilled because it is beneath our dignity it is wrong. When we feel something is owed to us just because of whom we are it is wrong. When we desire and immorally take more than what we actually need it is wrong. Contentment should be found in having our needs, not our wants, met. God has given us unique gifts and talents, not for our own elevation or gain, but to use to show His glory and the benefit of fellow Christians.

All desire the right to be autonomous and self-guiding, but that is not why we were created. We are God's by His creation and the life He has blessed us with. When we submit ourselves totally to Him, we then gain victory over the battle for our minds.

---

103   John 15:7 NIV
  104 Romans 12:3

IN THE MIDST OF BATTLE

As in all battles, casualties do occur in the struggle of life. Some are injured, crippled, and may even die during conflict. This does not mean that victory is not achieved; it means that we are in the hands of the Divine General who knows what the objective is and how it will play out. Sadly many are faced with unanswerable questions about the trials and pain experienced as the result of participating in this clash between good and evil. Many dreams and hopes are unrealized in life and the reasons are profoundly hidden. When these trials occur we are reminded; "And we know that in all things God works for the good of those who love him, who have been called according to his purpose."[105] We can only have faith that the Infinite One is loving and compassionate toward all who surrender to Him, and has the circumstances worked out for the final result to be graciously assured.

No matter the situations we face we are assured that we are never alone. It is written in Hebrews; "never will I leave you; never will I forsake you."[106] We are His and nothing but our own choice can alter this promise. We also read in Romans: "No, in all these things we are more than conquerors through him who loved us. For I am convinced that neither death nor life, neither angels nor demons, neither the present nor the future, nor any powers, neither height nor depth, nor anything else in all creation, will be able to separate us from the love of God that is in Christ Jesus our Lord."[107] We will never be abandoned by God unless we make that choice ourselves by not truly surrendering to Him in the first place. The only way we can become prisoners of war is by our rejection of God's truth.

During a heated battle individual warriors accomplish many mighty feats, but the battle is never won single-handedly. It takes a well trained and equipped army to stand firm as the opposing forces converge. It also takes a mighty leader to plan each strategy for the time and place for each engagement. Christians are to stand shoulder to shoulder, united in faith, and empowered by the Holy Spirit, to press on toward God's ultimate victory. We are to persevere until the day comes when the trumpet shall sound, and the Lord Jesus Christ returns in victory to gather us to Him, and we shall remain with Him forever.

---

105   Romans 8:28 NIV
106   Hebrews 13:5 NIV
107   Romans 8:37 NIV

POINTS TO PONDER

1. 1. Over what am I to have victory?

2. What does it mean to be more than "conquerors"? (Romans 8:37)

3. "Thanks be to God who gives victory through our Lord Jesus Christ". (1 Cor 15:57) Am I a victorious Christian?

11

PREPARE TO PERSERVERE!

All too often people have some long term, major goal they are set as their ultimate ambition. Some may call this a light at the end of the tunnel, or the point of satisfaction. They spend so much time and energy trying to achieve that one goal that they create for themselves a god. They may look forward to the day that their children are grown and they will have more freedom and money to "really enjoy life." Students long for the day that they receive their diplomas and can finally become self sufficient and independent, believing that by paying the price of completing school they deserve to be given a great job and financial security. For others it may be the day when they can retire, and the freedom that comes from not being tied to the daily ritual of work. Maybe their dream is the day of financial freedom which comes when they finally pay off the car or home loan. What they tie their long term dream to, all too often, is not what they expected it to be and the god they worshiped fell short of their expectations. Tedium can become the new schoolmaster of recently graduated students. For the retiree, boredom can become the demanding boss or errant child rather than freedom from work or the responsibilities of raising children. Finances are not as good as expected, and the lack of funds limits travel and vacation plans. All too often the sacrifices incurred to realize dreams were not worth the end result. Too late these people realize there is but one God who is worth their life's efforts, and self-worth flees with unrealized dreams. Too late the understanding that their futile efforts have not produced fruitful and soul fulfilling results is learned. Theirs is a life spent chasing illusions of rewarding aspirations without the tools or knowledge to catch them, and sadly they never really understanding their purpose for life.

EVERYONE CAN TRIUMPH

The same can be true for Christians also. As new members of the body of Christ there is often zeal to do the work of the church, but the feeling of inadequacy or unworthiness prevents results, and frustration may result. This goes back to the supposition that they are the ones to do the work. They do not realize that they can do nothing on their own that counts for the Kingdom, but it is the power of God furthering His plan through them that brings glory and honor to Him, and fulfillment to His people. The great stories in the scriptures lead us to believe that those involved were great and powerful people, possessing great wisdom and abilities beyond the norm. We look at the writers of the Bible as astute scholars blessed with all knowledge and wisdom. Have we forgotten which nation on the earth God choose to call His own? Have we forgotten to whom Jesus brought the Gospel? Have we forgotten with whom He dined and shared the truth of God? It was the nation of Israel He called to be His, and sinners and tax collectors He called to repentance. It was to the poor and down-trodden He gave the Gospel of Good News. And, it was a group of fishermen and uneducated working men whom He called to be His disciples. Jesus did not go to the religious leaders of His Father's people. It was not to the kings and princes that He came to announce the Hope of Salvation, it was the common, poor, and sick that needed a physician. To them He came and made Himself known through His teachings and works of great power.

God looks for humble hearts, those who have been beaten down or forgotten because of their social status or worldly prestige. God looks for those whose pride has been tempered by the lack of personal standing and importance. God looks for, and uses those who will not keep the glory and honor for themselves but instead give it to Him. God looks for those who are, on their own, incapable of mighty works, and through them, put to shame those who are proud and hard hearted.

That is why the actions we take and the things we say are not as important as our willingness to know God. To seek, have faith in, and obey Him in everything He asks, is the attribute He holds most dear. God is always searching for the right "heart attitude." That is why in 1

Samuel when God sent Samuel to anoint the new king of Israel He said to him; "Do not consider his appearance or his height, for I have rejected him. The Lord does not look at the things man looks at. Man looks at the outward appearance, but the Lord looks at the heart."[108] David's brothers were impressive physical specimens, and the wisdom of man (including Samuel's) would have chosen one of them as the new king of Israel. David, whom Samuel did anoint, was not of great stature nor did he have any external feature that would cause him to be chosen king. But, David's heart was pure and obedient and he was totally dependant on God for his capabilities. God knew that David would always be so.

When heart is used in scripture, it refers to the core of mankind's being, the innermost depth from which man's drive and will break forth. It is synonymous with mankind's spirit. This is the source of our passion and determination, and God seeks its surrender to Him and His purpose. A proper heart attitude refers to the state of abandoning self and to seek and obey God's will exclusively.

HEART ATTITUDE

The "heart of a champion" is a well known phrase to many. It refers to the winning attitude that never surrenders in the heat of a battle; a drive that never yields to cowardice or fear. That phrase has been given to race horses that struggle through pain and overwhelming odds to run to win. It is given to any number of athletes who will not settle for anything less than victory. It should also apply to every Christian believer who has given themselves to God.

In football it is said that there are 4 Ds to a successful team. These are; desire, determination, dedication and discipline. An attitude that exemplifies these mindsets brings an enhanced chance of succeeding in athletics and in the life of all.

When we desire something in our lives, we make a conscience consideration to choose to pursue that purpose. There may be several desires active in our lives as we are self-serving beings seeking to acquire what we fancy. Our desires may change as we see temptations the world and the Devil lay before us. This is the desire ascribed in our worldly living. The desire for God is profoundly deeper. It is He who chooses us first and inserts into our hearts a passion to surrender to His call.

This myriad of desires may be present simultaneously in our lives, but

108   1Samuel 16:7 NIV

at some point a prioritization must occur as to which should be paramount. As scripture says, we cannot serve two masters.[109] We must determine which desire is worthy of a life-changing pursuit to attain. The definition here is not one of simple desire for something which we have come into contact with or merely a fancy to pursue, it is deeper that that. This desire is one that we have researched and concluded that it is worthy of all our efforts to attain. Time has been taken to establish the benefits and potential losses. After such deliberation we have determined to commit to this endeavor. When we have the burning desire given by the Holy Spirit in our hearts, we commit ourselves to God's principles with determination, fervor, and unrelenting zeal, by choosing to surrender ourselves to Jesus Christ and follow His pathway of holy living.

With firm resolution we make the determination to follow God. Becoming dedicated wholly and earnestly to fulfill the deep desire of our hearts, we yield our wills to the leading of the Holy Spirit. Through His inspiration we become vessels set aside for the purposes for which we were created. This dedication becomes the principal purpose for living and our passionate pursuit. However, we are pitifully weak and our inherent proclivity to sin prevents us, on our own, from remaining faithful throughout our lives. Thankfully the Holy Spirit graciously aides in our walk by clinging to us when we are apt to let go, by strengthening our dedication.

We are called to be Disciples of Christ, and to practice discipline in our walk with Him. The root of both disciple and discipline pertains to being a pupil or having training or instruction. Persevering in the face of adversity requires a great deal of discipline. The more we know of God and are taught by Him the more we can trust and obey Him. Discipline encompasses several actions carried out in resolute determination to fulfill our purpose. Discipline requires faith to persist in doing good. Discipline requires strength to obey the leading of the Holy Spirit and in standing in resistance to evil. Discipline is required to continue the training of our mental, moral, and physical powers by instruction, exercise, and self control. Thankfully, we again are lead and encouraged by the presence of the Holy Spirit, Who continually points us toward becoming the likeness of Jesus Christ.

Practicing discipline causes us to continue seeking and learning in the faith we have proclaimed, and to utilize this knowledge by acting and responding toward God's creation accordingly. Every facet of our lives

---

109   Matthew 6:24

will be called to change in the way we interact with and approach others, with the aspiration of revealing Jesus Christ to the world in which we have been placed.

Once we have been filled with the desire for God, have made the determination to live for God, remain dedicated to do the will of God, and practice the discipline of God, we will have the proper heart attitude for Him to use us mightily.

LIVING WITH PROPER HEART ATTITUDE

Living with a proper heart attitude is an ongoing process, beginning the day we are reborn with the Holy Spirit until the day we stand face to face with God. It is not a singular event but a continual practice. It entails submission and obedience to the will and guidance of our Heavenly Father, and becoming holy and pure as one of His elect.

Submission occurs as we surrender all we are and all we have to His divine authority. All the hopes, dreams, and plans that we have previously been applying our efforts towards must now be replaced with the plans that God reveals to us. The prioritizing with which we have been accustomed is insignificant to our lives and well-being when compared to the glorious mission God has long been planning and equipping us to accomplish.

Not only are our aspirations in need of surrender, but everything we are and possess also. Our jobs, families, possessions, and resources must all be surrendered to our loving God who has more and better courses of action to show us. If God is not the top priority in our lives, He is not our God. We make an idol out of what ever comes before Him and we blindly serve this false god

Submission is not an unpleasant task, if it is done with faith and joy knowing that the purpose we were created for is coming to pass, and if it is done out of our love for God. Submission gives total security to our hearts and surety that the One Who has all authority in Heaven and on Earth loves us and from His bounty will grant our needs.

The proper heart attitude is only possible through absolute obedience to the leading of the Holy Spirit and ordinances of God. The leading of the Holy Spirit may seem to be in total opposition to out normal thoughts, even bordering on complete foolishness. The scripture says "For the foolishness of God is wiser than man's wisdom, and the weakness of God is stronger than man's strength."[110] His arrangement of our circumstances along with His perfect timing calls for prompt action in our obedience to Him. As always our loving Heavenly Father allows choice. We have the freedom to choose, but not the ability to choose the consequences which our choice brings. Choosing to obey brings the blessings He has for all is children. Choosing disobedience results in separation from Him and His divine glory.

Often is heard, "if I only knew the will of God, I would obey." Most of the will of God has been already revealed through scripture. The history of the Hebrew people, as recorded in the Old Testament, is overflowing with God's attempt to teach them His laws and ordinances on a myriad of topics. From moral conduct to business dealings, He spoke through prophets He sent. From the treatment of enemies to the treatment of families, He laid forth His ways repeatedly through those He touched with His Spirit. Not only did He give the way to be in relationship with Him, but He also explained the fearful consequences that would result from insubordination.

In due time, God tried to instruct His people further by coming in human form through Jesus Christ.[111] He displayed the very nature and character of the Heavenly Father and taught the way to live in His will.

These parts of God's will are readily available to all who read the scriptures. It is true that some of the private decisions we face are not found in scripture, but they are available through the Holy Spirit for those who continue to ask, seek, and knock. By being faithful in obedience to the obvious edicts of God, we grow to be in a position that allows the Holy Spirit to lead us through various doors of opportunity, or denial of such, as to become evident to discerning eyes. Through our God given character and abilities we can be aware of our personal mission when we compare it to the truth revealed in scripture. We cannot forget the personal connection available through prayer, both our own and that of a caring fellow member of Christ's body. In His perfect time and manner, God will disclose everything for us to obey.

HOLINESS AND PURITY

Holiness and purity go hand in hand in reference to a proper heart attitude. Holiness describes our state of being as we surrender ourselves

---

110   I Corinthians 1:25 NIV
111   Philippians 2:6-8

fully to God. We set ourselves apart from our worldly existence for a single purpose, that is, to become a vessel reserved for, and owned by, God. Holy does not imply absence of sin in our lives as that is not always realistic, but it means choosing to yield to God's higher purpose for us. In the scriptures we read "I am the LORD your God; consecrate yourselves and be holy, because I am holy."[112] God wasn't telling the Hebrew nation that they had to be perfect; He was saying that if they would surrender to His purpose (be consecrated) and faithfully follow Him, *He* would make them holy. They would become His holy people, a nation of priests through whom all the world would know and worship Him.

The dictionary lists several definitions for "purity". Among them are freedom from mixture, cleanliness-freedom from foulness, freedom from guilt, and freedom from improper motives. In our context, freedom from mixture means holding fast to the truths revealed by God through scripture and prophets. His truth is relevant to the essence of man through all the ages, and any deviation or diluting is an evil wrought by Satan.

Cleanliness or freedom from foulness is found in our living in the light of God, removed from the stench and filthiness of the dark. God is the source of all good, all righteousness, and everything proper for our journey with Him. Freedom from guilt can only come through God's process of redemption by the blood shed by Christ at Cavalry. Only by the actions He has already taken are we free from the guilt of past sins, and all we are yet to commit. Freedom from improper motives is paramount when talking about proper heart attitudes. The only correct motives can be to further the kingdom of God, and bring glory and honor to Him by exemplifying Jesus Christ through our lives.

Jesus said "But store up for yourselves treasures in heaven, where moth and rust do not destroy, and where thieves do not break in and steal. For where your treasure is, there your heart will be also."[113] Living in holiness and purity keeps our eyes looking toward heaven to where our treasures are securely kept. This manner of living also keeps us prepared for the imminent return of Jesus Christ in all His majesty.

GOD CAN USE US

The amount of teaching, training, and experience is secondary to the heart attitude of any Christian. Surely it is good to seek knowledge have

---

112   Leviticus 11:44 NIV
113   Matthew 6:20 NIV

practical experience when following the leading of God, but the love and faithfulness of the inner being is paramount in the eyes of the Lord for using His children to execute His will. When we are willing to accept His prompting and offer ourselves to be His instruments for carrying on a task, He will unhesitatingly empower us to be successful. It doesn't matter where we are in our walk with Him or how we have done in the past, a willing, loving attitude enables miracles to happen.

The maturity we attain in our Christian walk is also secondary to the proper heart attitude. The only part during our Christian life that is instantaneous (except for God exercising His will through Divine intervention) is at the time of our salvation, and the Holy Spirit enters us. Even as we realize our wretched state from living in sin, we assume the posture of lowering ourselves and elevating God to His righteous position, thus starting our experience of having the proper heart attitude. The development of our faith and knowledge affects the rest of our mortal lives as we learn about, and who God really is. Because of this, we don't suddenly awake one day and say "I've made it. Now I can go forth and fulfill my purpose and mission of God." Every second of every day we have the opportunity to seek God and answer yes to His leading.

We are told "All men will hate you because of me, but he who perseveres to the end will be saved."[114] What ever temptation or persecution we face in our lives, we are to have the utmost confidence in our God and still approach Him with the proper heart attitude; the courage to overcome through His power; the love to seek those who are lost; and the innocence to approach our loving Heavenly Father as a child.[115] While facing any obstacle overwhelming or small, we are to fast and pray, petitioning Him for His guidance and favor. We humbly seek His perfect will, and unhesitatingly obey at any cost. With the Eternal God for us, who can be against us?[116]

What then is perseverance? Perseverance is holding fast to the hope, joy, and victory of our God in all the circumstances of our lives through faith and trust in is mighty love and ability. It means to maintain a heart attitude which allows Him to use us to suit His purpose and thereby obtain everything He holds for us. It means to reveal Jesus Christ in every venue in which we find ourselves, and finally it means to reside in His glorious presence forever.

---

114   Mark 13:13 NIV
115   Matthew 18:2-4
116   Romans 8:31-32

POINTS TO PONDER

1. How are perseverance and faithfulness connected?

2. How does my attitude/faith need to be enhanced so that I may persevere?

3. Is perseverance as a Christian :
    a. A responsibility
    b. A privilege?
    c. A pleasure
    d. All of the above

Why?

12

LIVE PREPARED!

Living is so much more than just being alive. God has given to us the ability to experience His bountiful creation through our five senses. He has given us minds to wonder and reason that which we sense. He has given us the desire and ability to relate with Him and others, and the ability to love. It is sad to think that many in this world do not fully live, but merely just survive. Without the knowledge and reality of our Creator being fully involved with us we can never understand our purpose for living. Without Him we merely seek to satisfy the desires and lusts of our evil being. We go through the motions of life without true joy and are never completely satisfied.

True living begins on the day we finally acknowledge our sinful nature, and humbly ask Jesus to forgive our sins and the Holy Spirit enters us. Jesus told Nicodemus that this is being born again, of water and the Spirit. From that point on while we are maturing, we begin to have the mind and heart of God. We begin to see His entire creation as He sees it, through His *agape* love. *Agape* is God's self-less, sacrificial commitment of affection toward creation and seeking its absolute best. It was because of *agape* that God created the universe, to be the object of His boundless love. It was because of *agape* that God created us to share in on-going creativeness of, and dominion over the earth. It was because of *agape* that He gave us free will to choose to return His love. *Agape* is the center of God's being, and to which we are called.

THE FOUR LOVES

Every term of affection we have must have *agape* as its source to be genuine. Whether it is toward a friend, family member, or lover, true affection and love can not be sincere without *agape*, the source of which is God. All three of the other Greek words translated into English as love must contain a segment of *agape*, or they are a shallow and possibly even evil substitute when displayed by unregenerate people.

"Philia" is the Greek word which means friendly or brotherly love. *Philia* requires commonalities between individuals to begin. Without *agape, philia* becomes a means of exploitation by anyone who selfishly seeks to further his own agenda. Only with mutual *agape* toward one another, friendships can be long term beneficial relationships which provide a healthy environment providing advantages to all parties. Helping, caring, and sharing with a sacrificial love eases the trials of this life and provides a peek into heavenly things.

"Storge" is Greek for the love displayed within a family. Its affection runs deeper than *philia* due to the blood ties and natural kinship therein. *Storge* is somewhat like the natural or animalistic sense of duty, or bond accompanying relationships within a family. *Agape* forms the binding ties of family in *storge* which directs the energy to be put forth insuring a healthy environment for children to receive adequate training to become mature and wholesome adults. Without God's *agape* in family bonds, the result is too often a relationship of convenience. We have all seen marriages which are cold and pragmatic, and in which children are a burden. When we see the example of God as the Father and the relationship of Jesus Christ as bridegroom to the church, we all fall short of the love demonstrated by them in our own marriages. In *storge* as God intended, we see a husband who loves his wife so dearly that he will lay down his life for her. We see a wife submitted to the headship of her husband, and being a joyful helpmate. We see them together as a single unit serving God and raising their children lovingly by instilling into them the wisdom found by loving and serving the Lord. Without the sacrificial love of *agape* we see kids tending for themselves while self-pleasuring adults care only for themselves. We see broken homes with children being torn between two parents who think only of themselves rather than the consequences suffered by the children. All too often we see hate and mistrust poison the souls of the innocent ones, which may continue through future generations. Without *agape*, families act as strangers met on city streets, or at best casual acquaintances.

"Eros" is the passionate, intimate love intended for the close relationship between spouses. It is demonstrated by the burning love between husband and wife, the deep desire to be close to each other. Without *agape*, *eros* becomes simple lust, the obsessive desire to fulfill the wanton cravings of the flesh. Without the commitment of marriage with *agape*, sensual pleasure becomes an animalistic craving for unholy sex. The partners involved in such acts are not loved, cherished, or held in high esteem, they simply become an object used to fulfill an act of passion or convenience. With *agape*, eros becomes a uniting force which blends the two individuals into one new creation.[117] They become partners in life sharing the pain and pleasure life brings with God as their unifier.

Agape is the perfect love of God. Not only is it needed and found in the three other loves, is in itself is the culmination of all the loves combined. We become sons and daughters of the living God when we receive Jesus as our Lord and Savior and surrender our lives to Him. As we become family, we see God's *storge*. Jesus said, "You are my friends if you do what I command. I no longer call you servants, because a servant does not know his master's business. Instead, I have called you friends, for everything that I learned from my Father I have made known to you."[118] In being friends with Christ we experience *philia*. *Philia* demands choice. As the saying goes "your can pick your friends but you can't pick your family". With both *eros* and *storge* there is an element of natural love included, that is, some commonality with the love shown by animals. With *philia* we choose those who share something in common with us.

The passionate love of *eros* is presented in the gospels when Jesus called Himself a bridegroom.[119] His beloved is His church presented to Himself without spot, wrinkle, or any other defect.[120] This passion to be together and shared lives is the fulfillment of the eternal love of God or *agape*.

---

117   Mark :10-8
118   John 15:14-15 NIV
119   Matthew 9:15
120   Ephesians 5:27

PERFECT LOVE

When asked concerning the greatest commandment, Jesus said: "'Love the Lord your God with all your heart and with all your soul and with all your mind.' This is the first and greatest commandment. And the second is like it: 'Love your neighbor as yourself.' All the Law and the Prophets hang on these two commandments."[121] This love is not just *philia*, (although it may begin as such.) It is neither *storge* nor *eros*, it is *agape*. We as mere mortal men cannot generate *agape*. We can not love with the love of the Lord for His creation. We must allow the Holy Spirit to change us to have the mind and heart of God. Then we will begin to love with His eternal love and reach out to His creation with it and through it.

God has done everything since before time out of His love. He made creation out of His desire to demonstrate His love, and likewise He maintains it. He chose the nation of Israel to show His love to all mankind. He sent His only begotten Son to live among us and die for our salvation to show His love. And, on judgment day, all who have loved Him in return will see His magnificent love as He receives them into His New Jerusalem.

We are to look at our fellow human beings and all creation through the loving eyes of God, but there is another area to thus look; that is at ourselves. God sent His Son that we might receive salvation and come into a right relationship with Him. This means that we are of great value to Him. Regardless of our self-image, we are important enough to Him to die for. We are to see ourselves through the eyes of the One who willingly went to the cross to suffer and die. God deeply loves us and this is how we should see ourselves.

This by no means gives us cause to over-esteem ourselves however. When compared to God's holy standard we are wretched creatures bound to death by our limitless proclivity to sin. When we have been redeemed by the blood of the Lamb, Jesus Christ, we take on His righteousness and we should see ourselves through this light, having no righteousness of our own. By this we should exhibit no pride or arrogance, just humble gratitude in being accepted into the family of God. When we see ourselves through the eyes of God, endowed with Christ's righteousness, we can love ourselves and all else with God's love.

---

121   Matthew 22:37-40 NIV

IN PREPAREDNESS

While living and reflecting God's love, we should live in preparedness for any of a number of eventualities. First, Christ may return at any moment.[122] We do not know when the Lord will return for His own. It could be at any minute for He comes as a thief in the night.[123] With our eyes longingly searching for His return, we live as if it could be this very day. Until that day comes, we continually confess, repent, and have our sins washed by His blood, while humbly obeying the leading of the Holy Spirit.

The time on earth allotted to us is known only by God, as He has numbered our days.[124] When we awoke this morning, there was no assurance that we would return home to bed this evening. Today may be the day that the Lord calls us home and our mortal life ceases. Today may be the great reunion with all the saints that have gone before us as we join them eternally praising our God.

Whether by death or by the rapture of the church, we will one day come into the presence of the living God. By living as if today is our last day, we continually monitor our actions to make them presentable to our Father. By treating others as if we will never see them again in this life, we will be more loving to them and attentive to their needs. By praying with the fervency of a dying person we will be undeniably honest and open with God. Our lives are in His hands and we should neither fear nor seek death, but we should live with the perseverance of an impending conversion to a spiritual being.

THE GREAT COMMISSION

The apostles were charged with the mission to take the gospel to the entire world, with the promise of the presence of Jesus accompanying them.[125] We too are called to share the good news of Christ. Does this mean that we should literally leave our homes and seek to find those who have never heard the gospel, traveling to the far reaches of the planet? In certain circumstances yes, but only if the gift of evangelism is given and a call from God is discerned. The remainder of us is to share the life of Christ in every environment we find ourselves.

---

122   1 Thessalonians 4:13ff
123   1 Thessalonians 5:2
124   Job 14:5
125   Matthew 28:19-20

Each of us has a unique set of people with whom we relate. Our families, schoolmates, work associates, fellow members of a club, and our neighbors are a mixture of people that differ from each other. We are called to preach the gospel to all we come in contact with. This does not necessarily mean to stand before them ranting warnings of hell and damnation for non believers, it means to project the image of Christ through our words and actions which demonstrate a difference from the rest of the world. We are called to show the fruit of he spirit of which the central theme is love. St Francis of Assisi has been quoted as saying, "Preach the gospel at all times, and sometimes use words."

Words come into play more as we are asked about our good works and the love of God.[126] [127] We may be asked how it is that we be peaceful in the mist of turmoil. We may be asked how we remain confident as others tremble with fear. We may be questioned how our wives and children so lovingly respond to others. It doesn't matter what is seen to cause questions to be raised, for it is then we proclaim the gospel. Depending on the depth of the relationship we have with those who ask about our witness, we should respond to them accordingly. We are to share the gospel with them and even venture beyond. We are also called to make disciples of all nations. This is considerably more than merely proclaiming the gospel, it also involves baptizing and teaching.[128]

In Greek the word for disciple is "mathetes" which means learner or pupil. To be a disciple, we must be a student learning of and from our God. It also entails having a passion to acquire knowledge about God, and also to understand Him on a personal level. A good definition of disciple is someone who strives to attain knowledge, but who also brings others up to the level of knowledge that he possesses. In this we become a guide and teacher for those we have bought to God's family. When we exhibit the fruit of the spirit and allow our heavenly Father to prune us, we can bear more fruit.[129] Good fruit contains seed that can produce more plants to also bear fruit. This is how being a disciple creates other disciples.

Baptism is a starting position for a new believer. Baptism in is an outward sign of God's impartation of His grace for the salvation of the one being baptized. It is the start of a new chapter in the life of the one being baptized by being joined to the fellowship of believers in the body of Christ. In Matthew 28:19-20 we are told …"baptize them in the name

126   Matthew 5:16
127   John 13:35
128   Matthew 28:19-20
129   John 15:2

of the Father, Son, and Holy Spirit". The Greek word for "in" in this sentence is "eis". This word denotes direction and is better translated "into" rather than "in". Being baptized into the names of the Father, Son, and Holy Spirit, starts the newly converted on a journey which broaches the fullness of all that God is; His character, holiness, and nature are just the beginning of the glory that will be revealed, and toward which the new Christian will journey. Our part in this blessing is to bring the newly confessed Christian to the point where he acknowledges the importance of being baptized and deeply desires it. When we have developed the trust of this person, we assist in his teaching to help in further maturation into being a disciple himself.

Many feel unqualified to teach, especially about the eternal consequences of salvation. God, through the Holy Spirit is the one from whom wisdom and knowledge are presented. We are to be the loving conduit through which the teachings flow. The scripture is the text book from which we share the truths and ordinances of God, and the Holy Spirit opens the eyes and hearts of seekers to this wisdom. We have all experienced teaching and shared ideas in our lives before. If not, we could not have received what we currently possess, which starts with the truth of our God and His eternal plan of salvation, and leads to discipleship. We do not need to possess a degree in theology to lead others where we have been, we just need to be loving brothers or sisters who can present truth and encouragement when it is needed.

LIVE THEN!

What does living prepared mean? First of all, it means acknowledging who we are and who God is. Then to understand that man on his own is a creature bound for pain, suffering, and eternal damnation. God as our Creator owns us[130] and everything He has made. In His great love and mercy, He has given the path to His restoration and renewal of life as He planned. If we but choose to receive His wonderful grace, life can become as He intended it to be. We become part of the group who has made the same choice, and we begin to learn and relate to them and God.

After our salvation experience, we progress through the remainder of our lives with consistent growth of knowledge, worship, and obedience. Knowledge is gained through participation in study and prayer. Worship is the continual awareness of who and whose we are by living to bring

---

130   1 John 4:6

honor and glory to God. Obedience follows as we apply all we have gained in knowledge, and through worship, to every minute of living. All this is possible through the presence of the indwelling Holy Spirit.

When we practice obedience we begin to take on the very nature of Jesus Christ and reveal Him to everyone in our surroundings. With this the fruit of the Holy Spirit is manifest in us and the gifts of the Spirit are imparted to us to edify and uplift the other members of His body. Through obedience with *agape*, we become the flesh and bone of God to flavor and light the world. Through the victory of Jesus Christ we become able to fight the fight of good against evil and persevere to the end in faith.

At any stage of our Christian life we should be ready to hear and obey God's call. Moment to moment we should be alert to any command or inspiration of the Holy Spirit given to further God's kingdom and bring Him glory through our loving obedience. Whether we simply smile at someone who is down, or call down fire from heaven to consume a sacrifice as Elijah did,[131] obedience should be presented as our living sacrifice. Don't imagine that everything God asks of us will be monumental, for the work of the Kingdom is found not by what we do or accomplish, but rather in how we respond to His direction. The results of obedience are seldom the way we choose or imagine, and will often occur with out our knowledge.

There is no set point in our lives that we are actually "there". Life in Christ is an ongoing experience of learning and loving, and it will be until the day that we pass from our mortal bodies, or Christ returns to gather all of us to Himself. We live in joyful expectation of the coming kingdom, serving one another and all creation with love.

Even so, come, Lord Jesus!

---

131   2 Kings 18:36ff